The Future of English Spreading Around the World

A Brief History of English Language and Literature

HIROMICHI NISHINO

RYUTSU KEIZAI UNIVERSITY PRESS

PREFACE

This book is a by-product of the lectures that I have given at many universities in Japan over the years. It is not just a summary of all the books on the history of the English language I have read so far, but a unique story with original perspective and knowledge of European culture, literature, and history that I have acquired through my life as a university lecturer. The theme of my graduation thesis was the writing-style of Hemingway and the theme of my master's thesis was Sir Walter Scott's sense of history. Therefore, I'm especially particular about English and American literature. Naturally, the tendency to literature is reflected in this book. But I believe that the history of literature and the history of the language are inextricably linked, so I would like to emphasize that fact and try to quote as many original texts of the literary works as possible. As a result, I was originally thinking of making an English book on the history of the English language, but I changed the title (or subtitle) to something like "a brief history of English language and literature." The English used here is American English, and the level of English is the general liberal arts level of the university. This is a record of English history that I would like many English learners to have, in order for them to acquire a more comprehensive understanding of the historical, linguistic, political, and cultural background of English. In addition, I will mention the future vision of English, as an ideal form of the global language.

One of the drawing rooms in Scotland

CONTENTS

INTRODUCTION

If we get a glimpse of the history of England from ancient to medieval times, we will find that it is a history of racial fusion. The country intercepted a new invader, fighting, defeated, and was finally ruled by the invader. The confrontation between the conqueror and the conquered continued, and then the country was invaded by other races again. There was a repetition of ethnic conflict and fusion, although it's the same island country as Japan, which had not been invaded by other races for more than 2000 years. Aside from that being good or bad, in Britain, individualism developed, industry developed, and literature flourished. Being prospered as a nation, England became the center of the British Empire with colonies all over the world. On the other hand, some people mainly living in northern England, got out of the country and headed for North America, eventually founding the United States. America has now become the leading nation of the world, whereas its homeland, England, is now a small country, whose glory as the former British Empire on which the sun never set, has faded. Still, England, the United Kingdom, affects the world, showing its new life-style, its new art, and its unique culture. The UK is driving the world politically, same as the USA. Many of the former colonial countries continue to use English as their official language. English spoken in various parts of the world is changing and developing independently over time, and sometimes it becomes far from the original English. However, nowadays, with the development of the Internet, a wide variety of English spoken in the world is beginning to settle down. In various countries, a number of writers whose novels written in English have won the Nobel Prize in Literature. While absorbing local words that are deeply related to the identity of each country, English is steadily evolving as a global language. The essence of the English language is that it is simple and at the same time it can accurately convey complex and diverse content. Its plain expression that is easy for everyone to understand is welcomed by many non-native speakers. The history of the English language is the history of human progress and it is also the history of the fusion of various racial groups with different values all over the world.

Conwy Castle in Wales

1. The Celts and the Romans

The Celts is one of the old groups of Indo-European people. *Celtic* was the etymology of *celticus* in Latin, meaning 'unknown (person).' They originally lived in central Europe. In fact, (the) *Alps* or *Donau* are originally Celtic words. Towards the end of the 5th century BC, they began to leave their homeland, and moved everywhere, making many dialects of their language developed. They were widely distributed throughout Europe until oppressed by other races. It is said that they were tall, blond and white-skinned, but now Celtic people living in Wales, Scotland and Ireland are often short, dark-haired, and dark-skinned. The reason is probably because they had intermarried with the earlier people of Britain.

Around the 1st century BC, they landed on the British Isles because of the heavy pressure of expanding Germanic tribes. They started to live in Britain and mixed in with the former people whose ancestry had come from the Iberian Peninsula in 3000 BC. They lived in round houses made of wood in small villages. They made iron tools and weapons. Some of them started trading with the Roman Empire. They sold lead, gold, tin, slaves, cattle, and so on. They believed in many gods, and Druids or priests had great power religiously and politically. Incidentally, the language spoken by the Celts in present-day Ireland and Scotland is called Gaelic.

In 55 BC and in 54 BC, Julius Caesar with the Roman fleet attacked Britain in vain. Then in AD 43 the mighty Roman troops invaded Britain again. An army of 45,000 soldiers landed at Richborough in Kent. They marched into the country and conquered every tribe one by one. Then the Romans built roads and bridges and forts made of stones. Emperor Hadrian decided to build a 120-kilometer-long wall right across the country that separated the two countries, England and Scotland. The wall, which is called Hadrian's Wall was completed in AD 128. The Roman legions remained there for almost four centuries, and almost all regions now called England and Wales (not Scotland) came under their control. The Romans built strong towns to keep peace and comfortable houses. They introduced a good way of life and a new language, Latin. British Celts in the upper classes became used to the new life of Roman ways, for instance, their laws (arguments could be settled peacefully), police, religion, and education. They enjoyed Roman baths and theaters. The Celtic words in those days that remain in current English are of course the mixture of old Celtic and Latin that Roman armies and merchants brought. To be precise, such words should be called Romano-Celtic.

The Celtic word for *river* survives in the river name Avon. *Stratford-Upon-Avon* is one of examples, which is famous for the birthplace of William Shakespeare. *Strat* is originally from Latin, meaning "street" or "road." The word *Thames* is Celtic, meaning "dark river," and the word *dubris*, or *dwfr* which

meant "water" in Celtic, became the place name, Dover, the port city in southern England, famous for White Cliffs of Dover or the Straits of Dover. After all, the British Celts or Britons could not leave many words in English today. But even now there are lots of place names connected with the Celtic language.

Roman Pharos inside Dover Castle

For example, London, the name of the capital city of England, is Celtic (Romano-British name was *Londinium*). *London* is originally a Celtic tribal name, but the word *lond* itself means "wild." Canterbury, the capital city of the Celtic Kent is also connected with the Celtic language (or Old English?), and it means "Kent-town." *Caea* or *Car* in Caerphilly, Caernarvon, or Carlisle means "fortified place" in Celtic. *Cumb* in Cumbria or Cumberland means "deep valley" in Celtic. Edinburgh, Deira, Devon, Bernicia are also connected with Celtic.

The typical and permanent linguistic remains of the Roman rule in Britain are certainly the place names connected with their major settlements such as the towns ending in *-caster*, *-cester*, or *-chester*. These are derived from the Latin word *castra*, for "camp," or "military camp." The word later meant any walled and fortified, inhabited place. Examples include Lancaster, Worcester, Chester, Colchester, Rochester, Portchester, and Winchester.

In Scotland, they still use the word *loch* (originally *luh*), which means "lake." Of course, *whisky* (whiskey), meaning "water of life," is also originally from Gaelic.

Celtic people are said that they are full of imaginative and lyrical spirits, and they are good at music or art. They love fairy tales and myths. It is a bit surprising to notice the fact that many of the excellent writers and poets in English literature are originally Celtic. For example, Jonathan Swift (the masterpiece, *Gulliver's Travels*), Brontë sisters (*Jane Eyre*, *Wuthering Heights*, and *Agnes Grey*), Oscar Wilde (*Salome*, *The Happy Prince*, and *The Picture of Dorian Gray*), George Bernard Shaw (*Pygmalion*, the basis for the musical play and movie *My Fair Lady*), Robert Burns (*Poems, Chiefly in the Scottish Dialect*, *Tam o' Shanter*, and *Auld Lang Syne)*, William Blake (*The Marriage of Heaven and Hell*), Sir Walter Scott (*The Lady of the Lake*, *Waverley*, and *Ivanhoe*),

Ruins of Hadrian's Wall

Robert Louis Stevenson (*New Arabian Nights, Treasure Island,* and *Dr. Jekyll and Mr. Hyde*), John Lennon (*Norwegian Wood, Strawberry Fields Forever,* and *Imagine*), and Sir James Paul McCartney (*Yesterday, Hey Jude,* and *Let It Be*). English people tend to be rational, reasonable, and practical, but the Celts, the people of Scotland, Ireland, and Wales sometimes have a vivid poetic mind. Enya (1961-), a popular Irish musician is also Celtic in origin as you know.

2. The Anglo-Saxons

From the middle of the 3rd century AD, the Romans grew weaker and weaker as the Germanic peoples of northern Europe invaded much more Roman lands. In AD 410 when the Germanic barbarians threatened their Italian homeland, the Romans finally decided to leave Britain to help defend their Roman Empire in Europe. Without the Roman army, the country was in danger of being attacked by other invaders.

In the 5th century, Germanic warrior tribes, the barbarians, came to England from the west coast of the European continent, across the sea. According to Bede (673?-735), the first English historian, in his *Ecclesiastical History of English Nation* written in Latin in AD 731, the Angles, people from Angeln, the northern part of Germany today, arrived and settled in eastern England in AD 449. Then the Saxons, people from the regions now known as the Netherlands and also the northern part of Germany, came and settled in eastern and southern England. And the Jutes, people from Jutland, presently Denmark, came to southern England. So, some of British Celts left their homeland and went north, perhaps into Scotland, others went west into Wales or Cornwall, and there were also some groups who went over the sea to the continent, staying in Brittany, France.

It is true that Angles, Saxons, and Jutes were so violent and savage that they took British Celts' lands by force. Some Britons had to escape from new invaders, and others became their slaves. On the other hand, some scholars point out these days there were also many peaceful immigrants from northern Europe in search of fertile land to live in.

Saxon burh (Saxon fort)

The Jutes stayed in the south of England and their mainstream tribes formed the kingdom of Kent in the 6th century and other tribes started to live in the Isle of Wight, which became part of the Kingdom of Wessex, which means "the country of West Saxons," in the 7th century. The Angles occupied a large region of the Midlands, moving north to Scotland. They took over two-thirds of land which is now called England and the southeast area of Scotland. They formed three kingdoms, Mercia, East Anglia, and Northumbria. On the other hand, the Saxons went south-west of Britain. They started to organize themselves into three kingdoms, Wessex, Essex (East Saxons), and Sussex (South Saxons). The size of the land that the Saxons ruled was one-third of present-day England. By AD 600, Britain was divided into seven Anglo-Saxon kingdoms. At first, the Kingdom of Kent was the most powerful but in the 8th century, Wessex became the most powerful and important kingdom.

It was the background of King Arthur's legend that the Celtic people had to leave their old land and were driven to a remote region, 'Celtic Fringe.' Then King Arthur appears. He is supposed to be the king of British Celts in the 5th or 6th century, who repels the Saxons.

The British Celts called all the invaders 'Saxons' at first, but later in the 6th century, the word 'Angli' was used to mean the whole group of invaders. Then 'Angli' became 'Engle.' The people from Germany were called *Angelcynn* and their language was *Englisc* (the *sc* was used for the sound of *sh*). By the 10th century, the country was generally known as *Englaland*, which means the land of the 'Angles.' And this expression is still used in modern English. Curiously Alfred, king of Wessex, called himself English in the 9th century.

Today we call the barbarian tribes in those days 'Anglo-Saxons.' But the word 'Anglo-Saxons' began to be used after the Renaissance (14th to 16th century period), when it referred to all features of the period, that is, tribe, race, culture, and language. As for 'Old English,' the phrase appeared in the 19th century.

3. Old English

Old English or the English of the Anglo-Saxons (in short, Anglo-Saxon) is the language that was spoken from the middle of the 5th century to the middle of the 12th century in England and the southern part of Scotland today. Mainly four dialects of Old English emerged, that is, West Saxon, Kentish, Mercian, and Northumbrian. There were no remarkable differences in grammar, vocabulary, and pronunciation in those dialects. When the invaders from the Continent dispossessed native Britons of their lands, they called the local inhabitants *wealas*, meaning "foreigners" in their language. The word became the Modern English word *Welsh*.

Old English spoken in the early days, around the 5th and 6th centuries in Britain did already have some Latin words, which the Anglo-Saxons had borrowed from the Romans before invading the British Isles. Also, before their invasion, the British Celts might have already used Latin words, because Latin was the official language of the Roman Empire. The Roman armies staying in Britain surely had been using Latin as well. When they left Britain, they left many Latin words. The words such as *belt* (belt), *catte* (cat), *cyse* (cheese), *disc* (dish), *plante* (plant), *straet* (street), *weall* (wall), and *win* (wine) are all originally from Latin and were included in the Old English vocabulary. About 400-500 Latin words began to appear in Old English manuscripts. It is said the total number of Latin words in present-day English is about 200 words. Certainly, the number includes Latin words which later Christian missionaries brought. In summary, there were 400-500 Latin words in Old English. Some were brought in by the Romans first, then by the Anglo-Saxons, and others by

Christian missionaries.

Most Anglo-Saxon settlers could not read or write. They did not have a developed society. They were just hunting, fishing, farming (growing vegetables, barley, and wheat), and drinking. They were passionate about fighting. They respected the person who was killed in battle. They built their villages surrounded by high walls made from split tree trunks. They lived in small wooden houses, also kept horses, hawks, and hounds. Nevertheless, there were some people who could read and write.

St. Augustine

They used runes, the runic alphabet. These were 24 letters which had been used by the Germanic peoples in northern Europe. The word 'rune' originally meant "secret" in Gothic. It dates from around the 2nd or the 3rd century. No one knows where these alphabets came from. But maybe it is a development of one of the alphabets of southern Europe, probably the Roman alphabet. The alphabet we use today is originally from Greek. The first two letters of the Greek alphabet are *alpha* and *beta*.

The runic scripts could well have been invented in the Rhine area. Perhaps there were lively trade contacts between Germanic peoples and the Romans in the early centuries of the era. The runes were carved in stones or weapons and were often used to show the maker or the owner. They were used as a good luck charm or an ornament.

The arrival of St. Augustine in AD 597, brought changes to Anglo-Saxon life. He came to Kent from Rome with about 40 monks to spread the teaching of Christianity. The mission of Augustine had been inspired by the man whose later title was Pope Gregory the Great. When he was walking around one morning in the market of Rome, Gregory happened to come across some fair-haired boys about to be sold as slaves. He was told they came from Britain and they were not Christian. What was Britain? He was told those boys were called 'Angles.' He thought they had an angelic face and that such boys should be co-heirs with the angels in heaven. Gregory intended to go to Britain by himself but in the end, he sent Augustine to the land of the Angles.

Augustine and his followers would have been worried about the notoriously savage tribes they were trying to convert to Christianity. However, they were warmly welcomed in Canterbury where a small Christian community had already existed. St. Augustine converted Ethelbert, King of Kent, who became the first Anglo-Saxon Christian king. The conversion of England to Christianity was gradual but resolved peacefully. By the end of the 7th century, all the Anglo-Saxon kingdoms became Christian. As for Wales, the Welsh had already been Christians since the Roman Conquest. The descendants of Roman Britons living in Ireland had also been Christians.

Missionaries introduced the habit of reading and writing. Then in a little more than a century, the Bible and other large number of religious manuscripts were written in Latin. At the same time, Old English manuscripts (translations) were also written in the 8th century. Unfortunately, most of them were burned to ashes by the Vikings who came to Britain later.

The missionaries and monks made churches, and there they taught Greek and Latin as well as Christianity. As a result, lots of Latin words (about 500 new Latin words) entered Old English. Those new words were mainly connected with Christianity and learning. For example, *munuc* (monk), *mynster* (minster), *school*, *fenester* (window), *cest* (chest), *spendan* (to spend), *to dance*, and *tyrnan* (to turn). *Pope* is Greek, and Greek words such as *angelos* (messenger) and *diabolos* (slanderer) were transformed into *angel* and *devil*. Or some of the Old English words at that time, such as *heaven, hell, god, gospel* (originally meaning good news, god-spell), *holy, sin,* were given new meanings with a deeper significance. These words are typical ones that are deeply connected with Christianity.

At first, the monks wrote in Latin only, but then they began to write in Old English, too. They usually spelled every word based on their own pronunciation. But it may be better to say that the spelling was dependent on the dialect rather than on the individual. Different pronunciations of the same word co-existed from region to region because there were so many dialects. In the south-east of the country, for example, the word for 'evil' was spelled as *efel*, but it was spelled as *yfel* in other places. More than hundreds of such spelling differences existed. Of course, in those days, all the letters in a word had to be pronounced. For example, the letter *h* in *hring* (ring) was pronounced as it was spelled.

The difference of dialect originally comes from the different linguistic backgrounds of the invading tribes, who landed on the British Isles and settled in different places from each other. The area occupied by the Angles produced two main dialects, Mercian and Northumbrian. The former was spoken in the Midlands, between the River Thames and the River Humber, and as far west as the boundary with present-day Wales. The latter, Northumbrian was spoken to the north of Mercian, extending into the eastern lowlands of present-day Scotland, where it confronted the Celtic language of the Britons of Strathclyde in Gaelic, meaning "valley of the River Clyde."

West Saxon was spoken by Saxons, in the south of the Thames and west as far as Cornwall where we can hear the Celtic language spoken. Most of the Old English manuscripts are written in West Saxon, because it was the kingdom of

Wessex, which was originally from West-Saxon, under King Alfred, whose country became the leader politically and culturally at the end of the 9th century. However, modern standard English is not from West Saxon but from Mercian, since Mercian was the dialect spoken in the area around London, when the city became powerful and very influential in the Middle Ages.

Kentish was spoken by the Jutes mainly in the area of present-day the County of Kent and the Isle of Wight. In origin, the place name Kent comes from the word *Cantus* in Celtic, which means "border." Canterbury Cathedral, which is the head of Church of England today, St. Augustine's Abbey, and St. Martin's Church are all located in Canterbury, Kent, and are all listed as UNESCO World Heritage Sites.

The vocabulary of Old English was made up almost completely of Anglo-Saxon words, and about 70 percent of the words had disappeared from present-day English. However, about 100 most common words in Modern English that are often used in our daily life came from Old English. Examples include *the*, *and*, *can*, *get*, *person*, *child*, *house*, *eat*, *sleep*, etc. Other words which survive to this day are seen in place names. For example, *ford* in *Oxford* means "a shallow river which could be crossed," *ham* in *Birmingham* means "village," *ton* in *Brighton* means "farm" or "village," and *wic* in *Warwick* means "house" or "village." Four names for the days of the week also came from Anglo-Saxon gods and goddesses. Tuesday and Wednesday were named after gods of war, *Tyr* and *Woden*. Thursday was named after the god of thunder, *Thunor*, and Friday was named after the goddess of love and beauty, *Frīg*.

Old English sometimes made new words by putting two individual words together. For example, *banhus* (bone-house) meant "body," *beadoleoma* (battle light) meant "sword," *bōccræft* (book-skill) meant "literature," *hronrad* (whale-

Canterbury Cathedral

road) meant "the sea," and *sunnandæg* (sun's day) meant "Sunday."

One of the typical features of Old English is much more varied word order than present-day English. The words in a sentence in Old English appeared in a different order like other Germanic languages. In present-day English, the word order is almost fixed. At present, *A helped B* and *B helped A* have different meanings, which we can understand from the word order. However, in Old English people understood the meaning of a sentence from the word-endings. And these endings showed the subject of the sentence, or the object of the sentence. So, in Old English *A helped B* and *B helped A* can bear the same meaning. It is said that Old English was an inflected language, that is to say, the role performed by a word in the sentence was signaled by the word-ending.

Today, most of these endings were extinct. We can understand the difference between *A helped B* and *B helped A* solely by the word order. The subject comes first, the verb comes next, and the object comes last. But the verb in a sentence frequently appears before the subject, especially when the sentence begins with a word that means "then" or "when," as in *Þa ongon he singan*. (Then began he to sing). Moreover, verbs are sometimes placed at the end of sentences.

In Old English, there were so many different forms of verbs, nouns, pronouns, adjectives, and the definite articles. Especially there were far more irregular verbs in Old English than in present-day English. In Old English, there were around twice as many irregular verbs as present-day English. The past tense of regular verbs was made by adding: *-de*, *-ede*, or *-ode*. For example, the past tense of *libban* "to live" was *lifde*, and the past tense of *lufian* "to love" was *lufode*. In addition, nouns had three genders, the masculine, feminine, and neuter genders. Adjectives and articles changed with the gender of the noun. There were also the pronouns *wit* meaning "we two" and *git* meaning "you two."

Articles, prepositions, and adjectives usually stood before the co-occurring nouns, just as they do today. Sometimes the word order was completely the same as today. For example, *Hwat sceal ic singan?* (What shall I sing?)

4. The Vikings and Beowulf

There is one clear stream from Old English to present-day English especially in grammar, also in pronunciation, spelling, and vocabulary. About one-third of the words we use today are from Old English. The history of Britain is said to be the history of repeated invasions. Newcomers to the island country brought their own language with them and left a lot of words when they left. Namely Celtic, Latin, Greek, and the language of Anglo-Saxon, which is the most important mainstream of English. Furthermore, in the Anglo-Saxon period, there was another major influence of this kind. That is to say, another big linguistic invasion had taken place as a result of the Viking raids.

In the 8th century, Britain was invaded by the Vikings (so called by the Anglo-Saxons), or Scandinavian raiders, Danes, and Norwegians. Danes first appeared in 787. Since then, they came from Denmark or Sweden (Norway), and stole gold and silver from towns in northern England. Then they gradually settled there. In 850, a large Viking army attacked London and Canterbury, and the war continued until 878. In 866, the Vikings had seized York and ruled most parts of Northumbria and Mercia. Then Alfred (849-899), the king of Wessex, fought the Danish Viking invaders and won an important battle, and made an agreement with them to divide England into two regions. After that, the northern and eastern parts became areas that were subject to Danish law, known as the

A typical Viking figure

Alfred the Great

Danelaw, controlled by the Vikings. And the rest of England was controlled by the Saxon king, Alfred the Great.

In order to improve education, King Alfred decided to restore monasteries, and to make English, not Latin, the language of learning and literature at schools. So, at the age of forty, he learned Latin and began translating books into Old English. Later he advised to translate one of the important books in Latin into English, entitled *Ecclesiastical History of the English Nation*, written by a monk named Bede in 731 (mentioned above), now known as Bede Venerable or the Venerable Bede. King Alfred also ordered to write a history of England in English, *Chronicum Saxonicum* or *The Anglo-Saxon Chronicle*. It described the things that had happened in the past in England, and also what happened every year at the time when the writers lived. It was the first chronicle in Europe that was written in the vernacular language.

In the Danelaw the Scandinavian (Norwegian?) language, Old Norse, spoken by the Vikings and Old English spoken by the Anglo-Saxons coexisted. The two languages were used simultaneously and one important effect was that Old English became simplified. Many of the word-endings disappeared. Plural endings became simpler just as the *-s* endings were widely used, and many verbs which changed their forms irregularly to show the past tense now began to adopt the regular *-ed* ending.

Furthermore, thousands of words from Old Norse (ON) entered Old English (OE). Even now about 1,000 words of Old Norse remain in Standard

English vocabulary, with hundreds more in the dialects of northern England and Lowland Scotland. The words beginning with *sk-* like *skin*, *skirt*, and *sky* are originally from Old Norse. Some Old English words were replaced by Old Norse. For example, *swostor* "sister" (OE) became *syster* (ON). In some cases, both Old English and Old Norse words shared the same meaning, such as *sick* (OE) and *ill* (ON). Notably enough, the Old Norse usage of the verb ending *-s* for the third person, singular, and present tense began to be

The Venerable Bede

used widely. Three of the Old Norse personal pronouns *they*, *their*, *them*, gradually replaced the Old English forms *hie*, *hira*, *hem*. Also, the word '*are*,' which originated in Old Norse, took over one of the most important forms of *be*-verb in Old English.

The Vikings (Danes and Norwegians) left many words frequently used even today, such as *are*, *bag*, *bank*, *birth*, *both*, *bull*, *call*, *cake*, *die*, *egg*, *fellow*, *gap*, *garden*, *get*, *give*, *guess*, *harbor*, *happy*, *ill*, *kid*, *knife*, *leg*, *loan*, *low*, *odd*, *race*, *root*, *rotten*, *scare*, *seat*, *sister*, *skin*, *sky*, *steak*, *take*, *their*, *they*, *trust*, *want*, *weak*, etc. And also, they left many place names. More than 1,400 Scandinavian place names appeared in northern England. Over 600 place names end in *-by*, which means "town," "village," or "farm" in Scandinavian. For example, *Derby*, which means "many deer near one village," or *Rugby*, the name of the place where the high school that became the etymology of rugby football is located, are very famous place names in England. Others end in *-thorp(e)* meaning "village," such as *Althorp* and *Linthorpe*.

King Canute

Family names that end in *-son* suggest that their ancestors came from the home ground of the Vikings. Examples include *Jefferson, Madison, Jackson, Harrison, Johnson, Simpson, Wilson, Nixon* (son of Nicholas), *Stevenson,* and *Anderson* (son of Andrew). By the way, *Andersen* is a Danish writer of children's stories, and of course it means "son of Andrew," too.

From 1016 to 1042, England had been ruled by three Danish kings, namely Canute (reigned 1016-35) and his sons, Harold (reigned 1037-40), and Hardecanute (reigned 1035-37, 1040-42). In 1015, Canute started to bring an extensive invasion fleet to Kent. The English king, Edmund carried on struggles against Danish attacks. Edmund was so mighty that Canute could not have any other way but to agree to share England with him. But Edmund died suddenly in November 1016. Maybe he had been murdered, so Canute got all the territory of England. After that, Canute collected two other kingdoms, Denmark in 1019, and Norway in 1028. So, England became part of the Danish Empire until 1042. Canute, however, was not a barbarian nor an overconfident ruler. He was a sincere and pious Christian. He knew there were limitations to what one man could do. He made a great effort to keep his kingdoms in good order. He realized that once he died, his sons or relatives would not keep his three kingdoms nor rule each of them well.

A famous episode has been told about King Canute. One day, his courtiers had said that the sea would obey Canute with the dignity of the king's power. So, Canute ordered to put a chair on the shore of Bosham, Wessex. Then he commanded the waves to go back, and finally got wet by the seawater. Canute wanted to show that the king's powers were not limitless, that only Almighty God has the authority, and that how stupid his men's flatteries were.

When Danish king Hardecanute died, because of too much drink, the English people welcomed his successor, Anglo-Saxon King Edward, afterwards known to history as Edward the Confessor. He was the brother of King Edmund. After 25 years of exile in Normandy, he returned from France to become the king

The first page of the *Beowulf* manuscript (British Library Collection)

of England. It is said that he was more interested in religion than in ruling his country. He was, above all, a devout Christian and a person who sincerely loved peace. He remained single and had no children.

The greatest Old English poem that has survived is *Beowulf*. It is a narrative poem of about 3,200 lines. And nobody knows the name of the author. This epic was probably written in the 8th century or in the 9th century, although it was not actually written down until about two hundred and fifty years later. It tells the story of a brave young man from the 6th century southern Sweden called Beowulf. He goes to Denmark to help the king in trouble with a terrible creature. Beowulf finds the terrible troll called Grendel, fights against the monster, and kills it. And then, he also kills its vengeful mother coming to attack him. Later, Beowulf becomes king. And he fights a fierce battle and kills a fire-breathing creature to defend his country. But he is wounded terribly and dies. Beowulf is the first hero in English literature. Of course, it is the first English epic, showing elements of life and death, bravery, courage, strong spirit, vitality, the cruel nature of Northern Europe, and the benevolent Christian spirit.

> Wæs se grimma gæst Grendel hāten,
>
> mǣre mearcstapa, sē þe mōras hēold,
>
> fen ond fæsten; fielcynnes eard
>
> wonsǣli wer weardode hwīle,
>
> siþðan him Scyppend forscrifen hæfde
>
> in Cāines cynne —
>
> *Beowulf and the Fight at Finnsburg* lines 102-107[1]

> *This raging evil spirit dwelling*
>
> *In a wilderness, a moor, a stronghold*
>
> *Was called Grendel, the famed wanderer*
>
> *In the borderland where the monster race dwell.*
>
> *After the Creator proscribed him as one of Cain's descendants*
>
> *He lived in the monsters-dwelling-place for a long time.*

5. The Norman Conquest

Edward the Confessor (1004-66), the last Anglo-Saxon king, was said to be a very shy person. He did not like contention, lived only by reading the Bible, and wanted to live endlessly quiet life. He was single throughout his life, so he didn't have any children to succeed him. He might have been an incompetent king at that time, but now a way of life like him might be ahead of the times.

King Edward made his mistake promising the right of succession to his second cousin, William (Guillaume) in Normandy, France. When Edward died without a son to follow him in 1066, Harold, the son of Earl Godwin, who was the most powerful Saxon leader of Wessex, was chosen to be the next king. According to Harold, just before Edward the Confessor had died, the king had promised him to become King of England. However, William (Guillaume) claimed that the old king had already promised him the crown. William, Duke of Normandy in northern France, was also a strong and mighty warrior. He decided to take an army to England and beat Harold, who had already been crowned at Westminster Abby in January 1066. First, Harald Hardrada, King of Norway and Sweden invaded northern England at the request of Tosting, who was Harold's younger brother. King Harold marched heading north and defeated Harald's army at the Battle of Stamford Bridge. King Harald and Tosting were both killed by Harold in September 1066. Three days later, William, with 7,000 knights, landed near Hastings

William the Conqueror

waiting for Harold.

At the Battle of Hastings, on October 14, 1066, Harold's army was defeated by the Norman knights on horses. It is said that Harold was killed by the enemy's arrow shot through his eye. On Christmas Day 1066, William's coronation was held at Westminster Abby in London, and over the next four years, King William completed his conquest of England and Wales. William I (William the Conqueror) ordered his men to build castles all over the country, from which Norman barons controlled the towns and countryside. Later, a brave warrior and wise ruler, King Edward I (1239-1307) built many splendid castles in Wales as military bases for complete control against Welsh raiders. The Normans took large areas of land from rich British families. Each of the Normans had their own group of soldiers, and each of them gave land to their followers, so one Norman family ruled over each English village. Normans worked in the government and controlled churches. It is said that the population of England at that time was about 1.5 million, dominated by about 20,000 to 30,000 Normans.

William the Conqueror had a very great effect on the English language. Norman-French immediately became the language of the government, and it lasted for over 200 years. It is said that over 10,000 French words came into English; about 70 percent were nouns and most of them were abstract terms. French was used as an official language by the government, and Latin was used in church and at school; although English monks continued writing *The Anglo-Saxon Chronicle* until 1154. English was used by ordinary people,

The Tower of London

who didn't need to learn French or didn't want to do. French was the language of the Normans who had destroyed English towns and villages. English was the language that the British were proud of.

Windsor Castle

In England, French had been used in the court throughout the 12th century. Because having their lands in Normandy and other parts of France, Norman kings and barons who owned lands in England had to spend a lot of time in France. King Richard I, the Lionheart (1157-99), stayed in England for only 6 months as King because he was so busy with the Crusades. French was the only language they could use in the castles of the nobles, while English was the language of the rustics or countrymen. Norman French, a dialect of the Normandy region, was the language of honor, chivalry, and justice. Norman blood people (maybe 2% or less of the population) spoke Norman French, but of course, it was also spoken by some English men who wanted to become elites aiming for important positions in courts, law, politics, and trades.

A famous Robin Hood Legend in medieval England is based on this historical background. Robin Hood (Rabunhod) living in Sherwood Forest, Nottingham, is told as an outlawed Saxon aristocrat who had lost his land and opposes the cruel, Norman king's brother, Prince John (future King John, nicknamed 'Lackland,' also 'Soft sword' after the loss of Normandy and Anjou). Robin Hood had robbed from the rich Normans and gave stolen things to the poor Saxons. Sir Walter Scott (1771-1832) also introduced Robin as a character named 'Robert Locksley' in his novel *Ivanhoe* in 1820.

Walter Scott, a great historical novelist, born in Scotland, describes the relationship between Normans and Anglo-Saxons or the relationship between Norman French and English in his work, *Ivanhoe*:

> At court, and in the castles of the great nobles, where the pomp and state of a court was emulated, Norman-French was the only language employed; in courts of law, the pleadings and judgements were delivered in the same tongue. In short, French was the language of honour, of chivalry, and even of justice, while the far more manly and expressive Anglo-Saxon was abandoned to the use of rustics and hinds, who knew no other. Still, however, the necessary intercourse between the lords of the soil, and those oppressed inferior beings by whom that soil was cultivated, occasioned the gradual formation of a dialect, compounded betwixt the French and the Anglo-Saxon, in which they could render themselves mutually intelligible to each other, and from this necessity arose by degrees the structure of our present English language, in which the speech of the victors and the vanquished have been so happily blended together; and which has since been so richly improved by importations from the classical languages, and from those spoken by the southern nations of Europe. [2]

There is an episode that tells how French was spoken in the royal castle, Windsor. In 1348, Edward III enacted the Order of the Garter in commemoration of the victory in the battle with France. Since then, the ceremony takes place once a year in the St. George's Chapel at Windsor Castle. The formal title of the order is 'Most Noble Order of the Garter.' The strange name of the prestigious order given to 24 knights comes from an interesting episode: in the middle of a ball to celebrate the victory, a lady's sock fastener was removed and dropped. The lady then got very embarrassed and it brought everyone's cynical laughter. However, it is said that

Queen Elizabeth II   King Charles III

the king did not blame the woman's blunder, picked up the garter, fastened it to his left leg, saying:

Honi soit qui mal y pense.[3]

> *Disaster be to the one who thought this to be bad.*

He said these words in French which was used in England at that time, then the lady was saved. It is a typical example of chivalry, kind to the weak but brave on the battlefield. The term, 24 knights came from the legendary 24 knights of King Arthur. England's first and highest Order was born from such background. Since then, at Windsor Castle, if a new honorable person is being awarded the Order, there will be a grand ceremony in the presence of the King or Queen of England. As for the award for Japan, due to the relationship between the Anglo-Japanese alliance, Emperor Meiji was awarded the Order of the Garter by Edward VII in 1906, followed by Emperor Taisho, Emperor Showa, and Emperor Heisei who was awarded by Queen Elizabeth II. The current sovereign is Charles III.

6. Anglo-Norman English-speaking kings

French was the official language in England during the Middle Ages. However, English became more and more widely used by Normans. Many Normans married English women, and their children spoke English. The hostile blood of the Normans and Anglo-Saxons gradually blended. Henry I (1068-1135) one of the sons of William I, decided to get married to an English lady, and intended to harmonize Norman people with Anglo-Saxons. In 1204, King John, an Anglo-Norman king had lost Normandy and other French territories, and during the next fifty years, all the barons and landowners had to give away their

The Palace of Westminster rebult in the 19th century

estates in France. They began to feel that England was their homeland. Although the upper class continued to speak French, the language was becoming less important in England. Of course, their French was Norman French and it was not considered good by Parisians. The bad relationship between England and France resulted in the Hundred Years' War (1337-1453). During this time, anti-French feelings developed in Anglo-Norman people. A spirit of English nationalism was gradually molded. The English language was regarded as an important part of their identities. Besides, between 1348 and 1375, England suffered the terrible plague known as the Black Death. It came from China, carried by the fleas on black rats. Almost one-third of England's population of 4 million died. Many government officials, clerks, religious men, abbots, bishops, priests, and schoolmasters died, and they were replaced by the members who could speak solely English. Of course, the number of dead peasants was also very high at this time; as the result, there was a serious labor shortage and the position of peasants became stronger. The long war with France and the Black Death confused and destabilized the country politically. In 1381, Wat Tyler's Rebellion broke out. Wat Tyler was the leader of the rebellion. His real name was Walter, and although he was said to be a farmer, thinking of his family name "Tyler," his family originally might have been roof tilers. The armed peasants' rebels occupied London and attacked the hitherto impregnable royal castle, the Tower of London. King Richard II, then only 13 years old, had to meet Tyler and promised to vouch for his demands. During the second visit to Smithfield, London on the next day, Tyler was trapped and killed by the king. Surprisingly, it's said that the boy king used English when negotiating with the rebels (about 20 years later when he abdicated, his speech was given in English).

Gradually, working-class people came to demand better conditions and higher wages, which led to the collapse of the serfdom system. In the cities, as the general public, for example, craftsmen and merchants related to wool and cloth trade, became important, their language, English, also became important. Jumping about a bit in time, in 1362, the Chancellor had opened Parliament in the Palace of Westminster in English for the first time. Now, Anglo-Norman aristocrats became English speakers. After 1385, French was no longer being taught in all the grammar schools in England. When Henry, Duke of Lancaster (1367-1413) became King Henry IV of England, after Richard II's imprisonment in 1399, English people welcomed him as the perfect English-speaking king since the Norman Conquest (1066). Henry made a speech in English, his mother tongue, when he claimed the crown at the coronation ceremony:

> In the name of Fadir, Son, and Holy Gost, I, Henry of Lancaster chalenge this rewme of Yngland and the corone with all the members and the appurtenances, als I that am disendit be right lyne of the blode comying fro the gude lorde King Henry Therde ... [4]

In the following century, the English language took the place of the French language in the government. In the 15th century, some aristocrats couldn't speak French at all. During the Wars of the Roses (1455-85) between the royal houses of Lancaster and York, for the throne of England, most documents, sermons, prayers, romances, songs, letters, and wills were written in English. English had survived this way, but it had to change constantly as in the past.

7. Middle English Grammar and Vocabulary

After the Norman Conquest, Old English changed dramatically. Thousands of words from French came into the language, and many Old English words had disappeared. The language became simpler little by little and the English spoken in this era was named Middle English (approximately 400 years from about 1100 to about 1500). The word ending of Middle English became much simpler than Old English by losing most of the endings for its nouns, adjectives, and pronouns. The plural noun ending *-(e)s* was a typical plural form by the 15th century, though some plurals, for example, with *-en* survived as in *children* and *oxen*. Adjectives and nouns lost their grammatical gender, and *'the'* became the only form of the definite article.

The main change of verbs was about the past tense. Before, there were a lot of irregular verbs, but some of them began to end in *-ed*; for example, the past tense of *climb* was *clomb*, but the word *climbed* appeared in the 13th century. In the 14th century, most of the verbs which had entered English from French, also formed the past tense with *-ed*. Sometimes the change went the other way, so *knowed* became *knew*, though *-ed* was usually used. There are still about 250 past tense irregular verbs in English, but the number is only about half of Old English ones.

In Old English there were mainly two tenses, past and present. In Middle English, other four tenses developed, using *be, have, shall,* and *will. Shall* and *will* started to express the future. *Have* and *be* expressed the perfect tense at first, but later *be* was used for the passive. *Be* was also used for the continuous tenses.

When the word ending disappeared, people in those days had to put words in a particular order to express meaning. The most common order they used was 'subject-verb-object (SVO).' They also started using prepositions, for example, *by, from, in,* and *with* instead of noun endings. The loss of the Old English system of word endings resulted in the use of prepositions. Using prepositions and fixed patterns of word order, Middle English had made it possible to convey meaning in an easy way.

All these grammatical changes were made without any problems. From the 11th century to the end of the 12th century, they didn't write English formally. The official documents were written in Latin or French. This meant that they were free to change their spoken language very easily.

Until the 15th century, about 10,000 French words were taken into the English language. Three-quarters of them are still in use. Many French words came into every part of Anglo-Saxons' daily life, for example: *age, blanket, blue, ceiling, chair, city, curtain, dance, dinner, fruit, grammar, lamp, literature,* and *table.* New words about religion, law, science, nature, and arts were also introduced, such as *abbey, cathedral, mercy, crime, judge, heir, prison, punish, medicine, square, flower, forest, mountain, river, ocean, music, painting, sculpture, poet,* and so on.

French (F) words such as *people* (from French *peuple*) replaced Old English (OE) *lēode,* or F *pray* replaced OE *bid.* However, often both French and Old English survived as synonyms, such as OE *ask* and F *demand,* OE *blossom* and F *flower,* OE *board* and F *table,* OE *buy* and F *purchase,* OE *fight* and F *battle* or *combat,* OE *fire* and F *flame,* OE *hearty* and F *cordial,* OE *help* and F *aid, assist,* OE *house* and F *mansion,* OE *speech* and F *language,* OE *sorry* and F *regret,* OE *want, wish* and F *desire,* OE *wedding* and F *marriage,* OE *king* and F *sovereign.* Similarly, *answer* and *respond, room* and *chamber, start* and *commence, sorrow* and *grief* are all almost synonyms. The former English is casual and the latter French seems formal or public, respectively. Many French words came into English during the Medieval Ages. Some of them were replaced by new words in English, but others eventually coexisted, which made the English expression richer, expressing subtle stylistic differences.

Sometimes, the words for the animals in the fields were represented by Old English (*cows, sheep,* and *pigs*), and the words for the ingredients arranged on the table were French (*beef, mutton*, and *pork*), this meant, originally, the person who raised farm animals spoke English and the person who ate the meat spoke French.

Contrary to the disappearance of the typical Old English names, such as Aelfric, Dunstan, Wulfric, such names as Richard, Robert, Stephen (Etienne,

University of Oxford, founded at the end of the 11th century

Stéphane), John (Jean), and William (Guillaume) from France were becoming popular, and nowadays these are the most common English given names since the Norman Conquest.

New English words were made by adding the English -*ly* and -*ful* endings to French words, such as *gently, beautiful,* and *peaceful.*

During the same era, thousands of the Latin vocabulary entered Middle English again. They came from books on law, medicine, science, literature, and religion. There were many Latin words with new concepts not found in traditional English. Examples include *abject, adjacent, admit, conflict, incumbent, index, infancy, lucrative, ornate, pulpit, testimony, ulcer,* and so on. One of the important sources of Latin was the translation of the Bible into English. More than a thousand Latin words appear in the translation of the Bible.

The Old English dialects developed independently everywhere in England. The Middle English dialects were naturally affected by them and were similar to those of Old English. In those days, the pronunciation was so varied from place to place that it was sometimes difficult to communicate with each other. David Crystal introduces a famous episode in his *The English Language,* published in 2002, about a conversation between a farmer's wife and a sailor from London, which is only about 80 kilometers away from the place where she lives. The sailor asked for some *eggys* (eggs) but she could not understand him, because the word for eggs in her dialect was *eyren.* So, thinking that he must be a foreigner, she told him she couldn't speak French!

In Middle English one word was spelled in lots of different ways. There were more than twenty spellings of *people,* such as *pepylle, peeple* or *puple. Naure, næure, ner, neure, neuer* are variant spellings of *never.* Sometimes some types of spelling remained in some areas as one of the dialects, and other types of pronunciation survived in others. As you can see, the word *busy* is spelled as a combination of *b, u, s,* and *y,* but pronounced [bízi]. This is why the correlation between the spelling and pronunciation of English words is sometimes inconsistent.

The changes in orthography, the system of spelling, in this era was outstanding. The Normans introduced new alphabet letters, *j* and *z,* and they used *k* more often, and they also used *u* and *v.* They replaced the Old English runic symbol ʒ with *g* or *gh,* þ with *th.* They also changed *h* to *gh, cw* to *qu, sc* to *sh, c* to *ch,* and *ū* to *ou.* As a result, for example, *niht, cwene, scip, cirice,* and *hūs* came to be spelled *night, queen, ship, church,* and *house,* respectively. The *th* spelling came to appear occasionally in many manuscripts. In many words, they used *u* where we currently spell *v* or *o,* in such words as *æure* for *ever, gyuen* for *give,* or *tunge* for *tongue,* and *wunder* for *wonder.* Moreover, in some words, the letter *u* was replaced with *o.* So, now we have *come, love,* and *son* instead of *cuman, lufu,* and *sunu,* respectively.

In the 14th century, people wanted not only their first names but also their surnames. The growing use of family names increased significantly. Sometimes the family name was related with the father's name (*Tomson*; meaning "son of father Tom"), as in Anglo-Saxon times. In Scotland, *Mac* or *Mc* is well known as the meaning of "son." The Norman French also introduced *Fitz-,* meaning "son of." Other names signified the place where a person lived (*Hill, Brook*), or the town a person came from (*Burton, Milton*), or the name of his country (*French, Francis, Holland*), or his occupation (*Butcher, Carpenter, Constable, Cook, Fisher, Miller, Thatcher*). In those days a family name could be changed many times while they were living.

In the 15th century, the spelling of various words changed dramatically. For example, in verbs, the -*ing* endings, such as *running*, and the -*th* endings, such as *goeth*, as a marker of the third person singular present, appeared. And apart from verbs, personal pronouns *they, their,* and *them* were used in some parts of England. The 15th century saw an emergence of great invention which consequently helped spread the spelling of Standard English. In 1476, the printing machine was brought to London by a man named William Caxton. Since then, it was possible to produce thousands of copies of books. Caxton decided to use the spellings and words roughly shared in London, Oxford, and Cambridge, then slowly standard spellings spread. As a result, there are still thousands of words that are spelled in the way they were pronounced in Caxton's days. For example, the letter *k* in *knee*, and the letter *l* in *would* were pronounced at that time. From the 13th century, English was used more and more in official documents and in literature. More literary works in English remained from the 13th century than before. They left songs, poems, and explanations of Christianity.

Sometimes we see signs in London pubs with "Ye Olde..." to express the meaning of "The Old...". Originally, *The Old* was written as *Þe Olde* in the Middle Ages using the Old English letter thorn (Þ), but when *Þe* was handwritten, because of its resemblance to *Ye*, *Þ* was often confused with *Y.* Then *Ye* sometimes came to appear in late medieval literature. After all, this spelling arose from the mistake of misreading the first letter Þ as if it were a *Y*.

One of the pub signs we see in London

8. Literary works of the Middle Ages

The Peterborough Chronicle written in the 12th century in the South East Midland dialect, was one of the manuscripts of the *Anglo-Saxon Chronicle*, which contain information about the history of England after the Norman Conquest. The monks of Peterborough Abbey continued to write in English. Nine surviving manuscripts are still in the British Library and the other two in Oxford and Cambridge Universities.

Consisting of about 19,000 lines, *Ormulum*, an early Middle English religious verse, also exists. Written by a monk named Orm (or Ormin), it was a manuscript of biblical annotations used to preach doctrine at church. It is an important material for recognizing the pronunciation at that time, and it was familiar to monks and farmers who did not understand Latin. Only one copy of about a seventh of the material survived, which is now in the Bodleian Library of the University of Oxford.

The Brut, consisting of about 16,000 lines, appeared in the 13th century. It survives in two manuscripts, both of which exist in the British Library. The author is poet Lawman. It is worth while noting that *The Legends of King Arthur and the Knights of the Round Table* is introduced in those manuscripts.

The Owl and the Nightingale is a debate poetry using the South West dialect, in which a fierce debate is developed between an ugly owl and an attractive nightingale. Some arguments of the two birds are about sin, marriage, human weakness, death, friend, historical figures, and churchgoing. Anne W. Baldwin (Wisconsin State University) points out that the owl is Thomas Becket, Archbishop of Canterbury. The author of the poem is unknown, nor the exact date of its first composition. But it is assumed that it was probably written after the death of Henry III in 1272. Two manuscripts are stored at the British Library and the Jesus College at Oxford respectively.

In the 14th century, chivalric romance, *Sir Gawain and the Green Knight*, was written around Manchester in the northwestern part of England. The language used is a dialect spoken in the area, North West Midlands. The author is not clear. Three religious narrative poems *Pearl, Patience,* and *Cleanness* (which is also known by the editorial title *Purity*) are also said to have been written by the same author, including *St. Erkenwald* in 1386. The story of *Sir Gawain and the Green Knight* is very interesting. It was influenced by the legend of King Arthur, and the main character, Sir Gawain, was set to be the nephew of King Arthur, youngest of the knights of the Round Table. It was an extraordinary romance on the theme of the beheading game, the exchanging of winnings, the quest for the Green Chapel, the castle where Sir Gawain stopped for an inn of the night, the polite hospitality of the castle lord, the temptation of the lady of the castle, the etiquette of hunting, and what the ideal chivalry spirit is.

Piers Plowman is a Middle English alliterative verse written by William Langland (1330?-86?). It is an allegorical narrative poem with a lot of religious themes, mainly the true Christianity in life and the importance of Love in the context of Catholicism. Also, it is famous for mentioning Robin Hood tales for the first time. It seems that Langland was born in West Midlands because the dialect used in the poem is consistent with the one used in the region and there were also many names for places that suggest some connection to the area. He seems to have had a wife and children, and had made a living by reciting prayers for the dead.

The Cloude of Unknowing was also written to discover and understand the real relationship with God in the latter half of the 14th century. No one knows who wrote this work, but the author is believed to be responsible for other works, including *The Book of Privy Counseling*, *Deonise Hid Divinity*, and *A Letter of Prayer*.

Handlyng Synne (1303) and *Mannyng's Chronicle* (1338) are Middle English works completed by Robert Mannyng (or Robert de Brunne; 1275-1338), who was once a monk at the Gilbertine priory at Cambridge, then became a monk of Bourne Abbey at Lincolnshire in East Midlands of England. Mannyng's verse is often said to be vital and very colorful, being very exciting to the readers compared to other contemporary works. In *Handlyng Synne*, which consists of about 12,000 lines of verse, the author preached moral practice and theory. The doctrine was illustrated by referring to the events of daily life at that time. It is a valuable clue to know how the life of the British in the medieval era was.

Three long poems *Mirour de l'Omme* ("The Mirror of Mankind") in French in 1379, *Vox Clamantis* ("The Voice of One Crying Out") in Latin in 1381, and *Confessio Amantis* ("The Lover's Confession") in English in 1393, were all written by John Gower (1330-1408), who practiced law and was a dealer of wool living in London. Born into a wealthy family in Kent, Gower served Richard II and Henry IV as a court poet. Gower was a close friend with Geoffrey Chaucer. He was also a contemporary of William Langland and an author of *Sir Gawain and the Green Knight*. Shakespeare's *Pericles, Prince of Tyre* is based on an episode included in Gower's most famous work, *Confessio Amantis*. His tomb is in Southwark Cathedral in London. George Campbell Macaulay (1852-1915), a noted English classical scholar, discovered the only manuscript of the poem in the Cambridge University Library.

In the late 14th century, *The Travels of Sir John Mandeville* was written. The

King Arthur

author was not clear, and Sir John was supposed to be born and grown in England in the story, but in fact he was a fictitious character. This book is said to be written mainly based on various materials. According to the travel memoir, Sir John went to Jerusalem, Turkey, Persia, Syria, Arabia, Egypt, Libya, Ethiopia, India, China, Java, Pulau Sumatera, and so on. It is said that Christopher Columbus (1451-1506) was greatly inspired by both *Sir John's Travels* and the great *Marco Polo's Travels*. Actually, *Marco Polo's* was published earlier and had probably heavily influenced *Sir John's Travels*. The literary works listed above are extremely valuable in tracing the development of medieval English.

The name of King Arthur is a symbol of British history. The story of King Arthur and the Knights of the Round Table is one of the greatest myths in the country. King Arthur was a real king living somewhere in the south of Britain. He was the Celtic king, who died in a battle against Saxons around 500 AD. About 200 years later, his story appeared in Wales. It is in a work, *Y Gododdin*, a medieval Welsh epic, which is important as the oldest record of the legend of King Arthur. William Caxton printed Sir Thomas Malory's romance *Le Morte d'Arthur* (the Death of Arthur) in 1485. One of the most famous stories is the search for the cup known as the Holy Grail, used by Jesus Christ at the Last Supper. Other famous stories are *Sir Lancelot's adventure*, *Lady of the Lake*, and *Excalibur*. Sir Walter Scott published his narrative poem, *The Lady of the Lake* in 1810. Of course, there is no doubt that Scott adopted the title from *Le Morte d'Arthur*. Scott thought Scottish chivalry was the most important literary theme for him.

9. Chaucer

The greatest writer in Middle English is Geoffrey Chaucer (1342?-1400). Chaucer, who is called, "the father of English poetry," was born in a rich family of the wine trader in London. *Geoffrey* is a French-style first name. *Chaucer* originally means "shoemaker" in Old French (*chaussure, chauceure*). When Chaucer was a child, the Black Death attacked London, and he escaped death by a miracle. He survived, but many of his relatives died. Therefore, it is said that his father could take over huge properties and estates from them. Later on, a clever son of a merchant, Geoffrey, could work in the court as a page. It was an incredible start and a very rare case that was not realized by other ordinary people at that time. Educated as a squire, he became a government official involved in accounting, law, and diplomatic mission. In 1390, Chaucer also held a special commission as Master of Works at Windsor Castle. He supervised the repair of the St. George's Chapel of the castle. However, this chapel is not

the present famous building of that name, but at the location of what is now Albert Memorial Chapel, next to the current magnificent St. George's Chapel building. He is said to have stayed in the Winchester Tower on the north side of the castle. Chaucer was also a court poet, and he started his literary work as a translator. His first translation was French *Le Roman de la Rose* into English for the people of the court, especially the court ladies. He was good at Latin, Italian, and French. His artistic sensibility was

Geoffrey Chaucer

47

nurtured by the French literature and the Italian art. However, most of his best-known works were written in English, not in French, nor in Latin. His greatness is that, being an elite at that time, he did not adopt the language of French or Latin, but that of the language used by the common people in England. He had a genuine literary sense and valued the more manly and expressive Anglo-Saxon language. He thought English was his mother tongue and it was a national language. Chaucer used the dialect of East Midlands, especially London-based English, which was also spoken in the area of Oxford and Cambridge. Those areas formed a triangle, which was the center of politics, commerce, learning, and culture of England. After all, the English spoken in the London-Oxbridge Triangle developed into the modern Standard English. Chaucer used many words from French. His masterpiece, *The Canterbury Tales*, was written in the 1390s, composed of more than 17,000 lines, by using 20-25 percent of French words. It begins with the following famous lines of the Prologue:

> Whan that Aprill, with his shoures soote
> The droghte of March hath perced to the roote,
> And bathed every veyne in swich licuor
> Of which vertu engendred is the flour,
>
> ....
>
> Thanne longen folk to goon on pilgrimages,
> And palmeres for to seken straunge strondes,[5]
>
> ....
>
> *When April with its showers sweet*
> *The drought of March has pierced to the root*
> *And bathed every vein in such liquid*

Of which virtue engendered is the flower

....

Then folks long to go on pilgrimages
And palmers (long) to seek strange strands

....

The Canterbury Tales (ME, *Tales of Caunterbury*) is a collection of episodes told by the people of different classes traveling together from Southwark in London to Canterbury. This idea is based on *Decameron* written by Giovanni Boccaccio (1313-75), a poet and writer of the Italian Renaissance. The work of *Decameron* is a collection of 100 short stories in which 10 men and women talk about lovely episodes connected with people of all levels from royal aristocrats to the poor. In *The Canterbury Tales*, the characters also tell various stories. They told to each other on the way to their destination, Canterbury Cathedral. Those pilgrims had many kinds of occupations such as a wife of Bath, knight, miller, cook, man of law, friar, clerk (a student of Oxford), merchant, squire, franklin, physician, shipman, prioress, nun's priest, nun, parson, monk, and so on. Chaucer describes medieval people's way of thinking and behaviors ironically or satirically. After all, his point of view is concentrated in the interest in humans.

By the end of the 15th century, English was to be spoken and read by many people. The language became more matured and richer as a mother tongue, and eventually reached the climax. In the next century, a great genius of English literature, William Shakespeare appeared.

10. Modern English

The 16th century in Europe was a major turning point that would completely transform the world. In 1510, Copernicus (1473-1543) publicized the heliocentric theory: the sun is the center of the solar system and the earth is moving, not the sun. Galileo Galilei (1569-1642) appreciated the theory. There is a famous anecdote that Galileo said, "The earth is still moving," after being convicted in 1633. The 16th century was also the dawn of the Age of Great Voyages. Many

Henry VIII built the Queen's House inside the Tower of London

Europeans, especially Portuguese and Spanish began to explore Africa and Asia. Christopher Columbus (1451?-1506) was the first European to land in America in 1492. Then England, France, and the Netherlands began to explore North America. Sir Francis Drake (1543-96) was the first Englishman to sail around the world. That was the time when England was becoming more important in the world. At that time England was ruled by Queen Elizabeth I (1533-1603) and in her reign, the playwright Shakespeare appeared. Moreover England defeated the Spanish Armada in 1588. Elizabeth I, known as the Virgin Queen, became a symbol of modern Britain.

Queen Elizabeth I

Now the English language needed new words to express a large number of brand-new concepts. At the beginning of the 16th century, Latin dominated the language of learning in Europe. It was more authoritative and much richer than any other European languages. However, with the growth of education and the improvement of printing technology, more and more people began to read books, and in England, they wanted to read books in the English language. So, many foreign language books, not only Latin but also Greek or Italian, were translated into English.

In the 17th century, some important scientific books were written in English. Sir Isaac Newton (1642-1727) graduated from the University of Cambridge and in 1665, he discovered the law of gravity, or the notion of gravitation, by watching an apple fall from a tree. He first chose Latin as the language of his study, but later he wrote his dissertations in English.

During the 16th and 17th centuries, about 30,000 words came into English from many foreign languages to describe new ideas, concepts, techniques, and inventions; about half of them are even used today. They came from Latin, Greek, French, Italian, Spanish, Portuguese, and so on. For example, *appropriate, atmosphere, benefit, chaos, climax, crisis, emphasis, encyclopedia, enthusiasm, excursion, expensive, lunar, monopoly, relaxation, system, temperature, thermometer, virus* from Latin and Greek. *Battery, colonel, detail, duel, entrance, grotesque, muscle, pioneer, and volunteer* from French. *Balcony, carnival, design, lottery, opera, solo, and volcano* from Italian.

Moreover, since many British had gone abroad and they visited lots of places, new words were added to English, for example, *tomato* came from Mexican, *banana* from African, *coffee* and *kiosk* from Turkish, *caravan* from Persian, *harem* from Arabic, and *shogun* from Japanese. The English language was enriched in this way.

By the way, Latin was still used in the church at that time, but it was not used by ordinary people in everyday life. However, Latin or the words derived from Latin are still widely used as academic terms, such as in the fields of medicine, natural science, the humanities, mathematics, and philosophy.

New words were also added to the English language in other ways. People were adventurous with language, and they used verbs as nouns, or nouns as verbs, or made adjectives from nouns such as *shady* from the word *shade*. They also made new words by adding prefixes and suffixes, such as *forename, uncomfortable, straightness,* and *investment*. They made new compounds by putting two words together such as *chairman* and *Frenchwoman*.

11. Shakespeare

Enjoying the theater was very popular in Queen Elizabeth I's reign (1558-1603). In 1567, the first theater called The Red Lion was built in London. Then, other theaters like the Theatre, the Fortune, the Swan, and the Globe were built. In those days, all the women's parts were played by young male actors. Sometimes, they used animal blood in scenes where actors kill a person, to make it look more realistic.

William Shakespeare (1564-1616) was born in Stratford-upon-Avon, England. He became an actor and playwright in London and then built the Globe Theatre in 1599. Later, he is said that he's not only a representative playwright in the 16th century English Renaissance play, but also the greatest writer of English literature who ever lived. One great thing about him is that modern writers generally have a vocabulary of around 6,000 in their books, but Shakespeare has a vocabulary of over 21,000 different words. His work is said to be a fountain of words or a rhapsody of words. Another great thing about his talent was the combination of words. It created completely new meanings by connecting words that were originally not connected. Sometimes they had opposite meanings. For example, *cold comfort* (not to rely on anything), *a foregone conclusion* (the obvious conclusion from the beginning), *the long and short of it* (after all), *have a tongue in one's head* (be careful with your mouth), *an*

William Shakespeare

Inside the restored Globe Theatre in London

eyesore (disturbing), *a blinking idiot* (a dammed fool, a big idiot), *more in sorrow than anger, I must be cruel, only to be kind*, etc. The impact of Shakespeare's work on subsequent world literature is immense. It is said that he covers almost all the subjects of literary works after that. The themes of his work include national significance, loyalty, justice, crime, family problem, the relationship between parents and children, addiction to the mother, love, romance, adventure, friendship, racial discrimination, betrayal, suicide, revenge, ghost, existence (being), and individualism. The vast works of his plays and poems are still performed all over the world, and also, they are important sources of linguistics.

> *Ben*. Come, he hath hid himself among these trees.
> To be consorted with the humorous night:
> Blind is his love, and best befits the dark.
> *Mer*. If love be blind, love cannot hit the mark.[6]

Romeo and Juliet (1595)

> To be, or not to be, — that is the question:—
> Whether 'tis nobler in the mind to suffer
> The slings and arrows of outrageous fortune,
> Or to take arms against a sea of troubles,
> And by opposing end them? —To die, —to sleep,—

No more; and by a sleep to say we end

The heart-ache and the thousand natural shocks

The flesh is heir to, — 'tis a consummation

Devoutly to be wish'd. To die, — to sleep:—

To sleep! Perchance to dream: — ay, there's the rub;

For in that sleep of death what dreams may come,

When we have shuffled off this mortal coil,

Must give us pause: there's the respect

That makes calamity of so long life;[7]

Hamlet (1603)

Romeo and Juliet is a tragedy with the theme of "love is blind." Love is an opportunity to get rid of prejudice, but at the same time it carries the danger of losing sight of the problems that have caused the prejudice. The young couple should have listened more to the arguments of both families, as well as appeal for reconciliation between them.

Hamlet's famous monologue shows that in difficult situations, he does not rely on God, but seeks to solve his suffering on his own. And the existentialist prince who has lost Christianity finally meets a tragic end.

When Elizabeth I died in 1603, her cousin, King James VI of Scotland became King James I of England. In 1604, he ordered to translate the Bible into English. The university scholars or 54 top scholars were involved in the translation. *The King James Bible* (*Authorized King James Version*) appeared in 1611. It has a great influence on the later English language. 54 scholars and translators chose authoritative expressions. They were very conservative and valued dignity. They chose an old way of expression, or an older form of the word if there was an alternative. They didn't use new words that Shakespeare valued. The vocabulary number they accepted was about 10,000 different words, which looked backward.

In the beginning God created the heaven and the earth.

And the earth was without form, and void; and darkness was upon

The face of the deep. And the Spirit of God moved upon

the face of the waters.

And God said, Let there be light: and there was light.

And God saw the light, that it was good: and God divided the light

from the darkness.

And God called the light Day, and the darkness he called Night.

And the evening and the morning were the first day.[8]

Genesis, Authorized King James Version (1611)

In the 17th century, people wanted orders and regularity in their language. In those days, they spelled words as they spoke. So, sometimes they spelled the same word in different ways on the same letter paper. There were lots of chaos and confusion in grammar, spelling, and pronunciation. As a result, grammar books and dictionaries began to appear. As for dictionaries, the first glossary was in Latin. Then Latin-English and English-Latin appeared. Then

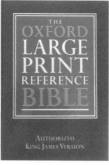

King James I and Authorized Version that the author bought at Oxford

Samuel Johnson in London

French-English, Italian-English appeared. The first English-English dictionary, *A Table Alphabetical,* was published by Robert Cawdrey in 1604. He defined about 2,500 hard words (loan-words) basically with a single synonym. This dictionary was made for the first time for the general public. In 1706, John Kersey's edition of Edward Phillips' *The New World of English Words* appeared. The dictionary is said to be the best of the hard-words dictionaries. It contained about 38,000 words. In 1721, Nathaniel Bailey, published his *Universal Etymological English Dictionary.* It contained about 40,000 words. This dictionary had been very popular in many editions.

Samuel Johnson (1709-84) published *A Dictionary of the English Language* in 1755. He defined or explained over 42,000 words. He introduced as many different meanings of a word as he could. However, his way of explaining was sometimes problematic and quite subjective. For example, *oat* is "a grain, which in England is generally given to horses, but in Scotland supports the people."

The history of this British dictionary compilation eventually completed as the *Oxford English Dictionary (OED)* in 1928. It required over 100 years and hundreds of workers to complete. The latest version of *OED* (2015) contains 291,500 major headwords. It contains even those that are no longer used. It also shows when the word was first used and how its meaning changed.

12. The Romantic Age in England

James I (1566-1625), who later published *the King James Version of the Bible*, succeeded his mother, Mary Queen of Scots, as King James VI of Scotland in 1567. But when Queen Elizabeth I died, he was invited to become King of England because Elizabeth was unmarried, and because James was a distant relative of the Queen. King James I of England (and King James VI of Scotland) wished for the union of Scotland and England, but it did not come true. Although the king was originally a Catholic, his religious position in England suppressed both the Catholic and Puritan. Under such circumstances, he aspired to publish *the King James Bible*. In 1605, Guy Fawkes (1570-1606) attempted to assassinate the king, but it failed. To escape the oppression of James I, a group of Puritans arrived in America aboard the *Mayflower* in 1620. James I, in his position of "the divine right of kings", was at odds with Parliament because he ignored Parliament and conducted politics. There were no major problems during his reign. However, James' son Charles I (1600-49), who succeeded James, received a Catholic queen, monopolized power and increased criticism of Parliament, resulting in civil war in which the defeated King Charles was executed. England was a republic without a king, and Puritan Oliver Cromwell (1599-1658) became Lord Protector. But after his death, his son Richard Cromwell could not control Parliament or the army and resigned as Lord Protector. Eventually, the Glorious Revolution took place in 1660, and the son of Charles I, who was in exile on the continent (France and Netherlands), was asked to return home and succeeded to the throne and became Charles II. However, after that, the unstable regime continued, such as religious conflicts and issues of succession to the throne. Finally, Parliament decided to invite George of Hanover, Germany, a Protestant descendant of James I. Thus, the great-grandson of James I became King George I. He didn't speak English and spent most of his time in Germany, saying, "Reign but do not rule." In 1745, the Catholic Bonnie Prince Charlie, who was in exile, rebelled with the support of France and Jacobite in Scotland. England was in turmoil for a time, but the rebellion was suppressed. Four successive kings named George followed, and the power of Parliament became even greater. During this time, there were many incidents such as the Scottish Rebellion, Seven Years' War, Anglo-French War in Canada, American Revolution, French Revolutionary War, and the Napoleonic Wars. Captain James Cook made three great explorations round the world, but he was killed by Hawaiians in 1779.

The triangular trade or the slave trade, took place among Liverpool in Britain, slave forts in South Africa, and the West Indies in America. During the Napoleonic Wars, Nelson won the Battle of Trafalgar (1805). Wellington won at Waterloo (1815), which ended the Anglo-French War. Since then, France has not turned its attention to Britain. During the Georgian Period (1714-1801), British Navy became very powerful and Britain nation became the most important manufacturing country in the world. With the Industrial Revolution, British society changed dynamically. The government was greatly influenced by large landowners and wealthy merchants. The country became stable, strong, and eventually propelled into the British Empire with many colonies expanded all over the world.

During the Victorian Age (1837-1901), British Empire grew and Britain became the richest and most powerful country in the world. It had the largest Empire, ruling one-fifth of the world's land and one-quarter of the people on the earth. During Victoria's reign, the British population grew from two million to six and half million. Prince Albert, who was the husband of Queen Victoria, died in 1861, and the widowed Queen became a symbol of Britain. As a result of the Industrial Revolution, sciences developed dramatically. The first typewriter (1851), the telephone (1875), the electric light bulb (1878), the sewing machine (1886), and the camera (1888) were invented in Britain. Military weapons progressed, and overseas explorations were further expanded. Scientific and technical vocabulary grows on an unprecedented scale. Meanwhile, at the same time, literature blossomed as if it could counteract the scientific universalism of the time. Focusing on the world of literature in this era, many important works in the history of English literature sprung up, especially in the novel genre.

However, we have to be careful about the so-called poetry of the Romantics, before mentioning Victorian novels. That is, many Romantic poets appeared in the first place, such as Blake, Wordsworth, Scott, and Coleridge. Then, after them came Byron, Shelley, and Keats as if they were cutting a weir.

William Blake

William Blake (1757-1827) was born in London. His father was a hosier from Ireland. William showed a talent for drawing from an early age and became not only a poet but a painter and printmaker. He feared for the evils of capitalism and commercialism. He opposed slavery and rebelled against authoritarian religion. He had high hopes for the French Revolution, but became disillusioned with the consequences. He looked forward to the

American Revolution and defended women's right to self-realization. He argued that "marriage is slavery for women" and became a pioneer of the free love. His best works include *Songs of Innocence and Experience*, *The Marriage of Heaven and Hell*, and *Jerusalem*.

Lord Byron (George Gordon Byron 1788-1824) became the 6th Baron Byron at the age of 10 because his great-uncle, the 5th Baron Byron, died without heir. In 1805, Byron entered Cambridge University, but dropped out of college. After debut as a poet, he became a social idol, and continued to live a decadent life. He published *Childe Harold's Pilgrimage* (1812-18), *Don Juan* (1819-24), and *Manfred* (1817) and so on. In 1823, he decided to participate in the Greek war of independence, but died there of a violent fever. He was 36 years old then.

Percy Bysshe Shelley (1792-1822) was also from an aristocratic family (his father was a baron and MP). He rebelled against his strict father and lived a bohemian life, denying established authority and morality. Among his best works are "Ozymandias" (1818), "Ode to the West Wind" (1819), and "To a Skylark" (1820). He became an atheist while studying at Oxford and withdrew from college after one year. The first wife committed suicide due to his infidelity. Shelley then married Mary, daughter of William Godwin and author of *Frankenstein*. In 1822, while aboard a custom-built boat in Italy, Shelley was caught in a severe storm and his body was found in the water. He was at the age of 29.

John Keats (1795-1821) was born in Moorgate,

John Keats

London. His father Thomas once worked as a hostler at the stables attached to the *Swan and Hoop Inn* in the City, and then, he married the daughter of the inn. Keats was ill in his childhood, and when Keats was eight, his father died in a horse accident. His mother Frances, just two months after her husband's sudden death, married another man, a banker, who ran away with the family's property, the following year. Therefore, Keats couldn't go to Eton or Harrow as the family no longer had enough money to pay the tuition. Frances got married again to an elderly Jew, but she broke up with him because of her illness. When Keats was 14, she died of tuberculosis. Keats left John Clark's school, and started working as an apprentice to a surgeon apothecary. In 1815, Keats registered as a medical student at Guy's Hospital. In 1816, the sonnet, "O Solitude" was published in the magazine *The Examiner* for the first time. In the same year Keats passed the exam to become a surgeon apothecary. However, he gave up on becoming a medical man and decided to become a poet.

Many of Keats' poems deal with the theme of beauty, and he is described as a "martyr of beauty." He often sought Greek mythology as a subject, leaving these words, "A thing of beauty is a joy forever:", "What is more gentle than a wind in summer?", and "Beauty is truth, truth beauty". Keats died of tuberculosis in Rome, Italy, at the age of 25. *Endymion*, who seeks eternal beauty, is his masterpiece.

These English Romantic poets from Wordsworth to Keats, changed the British way of thinking about nature, medievalism, individualism, and Christianity. Their achievements, in terms of language usage, subject matter, and target audience, laid the foundation for the golden age of novels, which envisioned the general public, during the Victorian era.

13. Wordsworth

William Wordsworth (1770-1850), a leading English Romantic poet, was born in 1770, as the second of five children of John Wordsworth, who was a legal representative of James Lowther, 1ˢᵗ Earl of Lonsdale. His mother, Anne, died suddenly of a malignant cold at the age of 30 (William was 7 years old), and five years later, his father, John, died suddenly of overwork at the age of 42. Not welcomed by relatives, William and his siblings were forced to leave their home and lost the foundation of the family. William went to Cambridge University but it is easy to imagine that he felt alienated by being discriminated against, based on status as a minority special scholarship student in a dormitory with many aristocrats and upper-class youths.

While in college, he embarked on a three-month walking trip to the Alps of continental Europe. After graduating from Cambridge, he hoped to pursue a career in literature, traveled to Wales, and climbed Mount Snowdon. In 1791, he went again to the continent (Revolutionary France). This time, he wanted to learn French and become a private tutor who would take the children of the upper aristocracy on trips to the continent. Eventually, he met a French woman, Annette Vallon, who was four years older than him, who taught him French for free, and they became romantically involved. Vallon eventually gave birth to their daughter Caroline upon William's return to England. After that, the Anglo-French War made it impossible for him to go to France, and his dream of teaching on continental travel disappeared. William published two collections of poetry, *An Evening Walk* and *Descriptive Sketches*, which sold poorly.

Before long, Wordsworth sympathized with William Godwin's *Political*

William Wordsworth

Justice and became an atheist, supporting the French Revolution. In 1795, he published a weekly magazine, *The Philanthropist* dealing with political criticism and political thought. However, 6 months after the publication of the magazine, Wordsworth decided that it was impossible to continue the magazine, and at the same time gave up on Godwin, disliked revolutionary terrorism, and distanced himself from left-wing communism. He sought the beauty of nature and the value of everyday life, deepened his philosophical contemplation, devoted himself to the inner soul of Man, the essence of nature, religious thoughts, and longed for a life like a recluse. In 1798, he co-authored with Samuel Taylor Coleridge (1772-1834) in *Lyrical Ballads*. Coleridge's gothic poem 'The Rime of the Ancyent Marinere' appeared at the beginning of the collection of poems, and Wordsworth's 'Lines written a few miles above Tintern Abbey' was at the end of the book. The origins of the idea were deeply rooted in the poor and oppressed real lives of the lower classes of the rural areas. The subject or theme of poetical works, such as, 'The Female Vagrant', 'Goody Blake and Harry Gill', 'Simon Lee', 'The Thorn', 'The Last of the Flock', 'The Mad Mother', 'Old Man Travelling', and 'The Complaint of Forsaken Indian Woman' are all the suffering and poverty of the people of lower classes. Main characters are old men, unhappy women, and unfortunate boys. At that time, there was no social relief for the poor and weak. However, Wordsworth sought salvation by getting close to nature, looking at himself, and deepening his thoughts.

.... For I have learned

To look on nature, not as in the hour

Of thoughtless youth, but hearing oftentimes

The still, sad music of humanity,

Not harsh nor grating, though of ample power

To chasten and subdue. And I have felt

A presence that disturbs me with the joy

Of elevated thoughts; a sense of sublime

Of something far more deeply interfused,

Whose dwelling is the light of setting suns,

And the round ocean, and the living air,

And the blue sky, and in the mind of man,

A motion and a spirit, that impels

All thinking things, all objects of all thought,

And rolls through all things…[9]

'Tintern Abbey' (1798)

One of the reasons why Wordsworth focused on the unfortunate and oppressed people as the subject of his work is that he wanted to alleviate his sense of loss: his family misery, losing home, and losing livelihoods. Or maybe he saw many poor people living in the countryside. Of course, Godwin's leftist ideology influenced him. Or is it natural to understand that in the context of human history, the transition of the protagonist of the work from royalty (and aristocracy) to wealthy merchants

Dove Cottage

and then to ordinary people? Or according to Wordsworth's thought, if you experience walking in the great nature that has a majestic and sublime beauty, kings and beggars are the same being, and there is not much difference between them as human beings.

Another important point is that in the 1801 revised edition of *Lyrical Ballads*, Wordsworth declared that the language of the work would be the ordinary language used by "the middle and lower classes of society." He would use the language used by rural people in the English countryside. This is a declaration that marks an important turning point in the history of the English language. To put it bluntly, taking this position, English can grow into a language loved and used by people from all walks of life. This is because "expressing lofty content in plain words" is the essence of the global language.

By the way, who started writing first about poor people as the main characters in literature? Its origins can be found in the New Testament. There are many episodes of Jesus Christ reaching out to the oppressed. Chaucer was influenced by the Renaissance and portrayed people of all classes of men and women in *The Canterbury Tales*. François Noël Babeuf (1760-97), a Frenchman, was a pioneer of communism. The word "communism" was derived from the Latin *communis* (meaning "complete equality"), and Babeuf rephrased it as "equality club" or "communist's club" in the 1790s. "Babeufism" was later replaced by "complete egalitarianism," and in the 1840s, it was replaced by "communism." British essayist Charles Lamb (1775-1834) wrote 'The Praise of Chimney-Sweepers' and 'A Complaint of the Decay of Beggars in the Metropolis' in *Elia, 1823*. Russian writer Nikolai Gogol (1809-52) published 'The Overcoat' in 1842 with a low status official as the main character. Fyodor Dostoevsky (1821-81) made his literary debut with a work titled *Notes from Underground.*

The French painter Jean-François Millet (1814-75) painted *Des glaneuses* (*The Gleaners*) as an oil painting of poor women in a rural area. Charles Dickens (1812-70), who later became a leading writer of the Victorian era, wrote many novels with poor boys as the main characters. *The Poor Man and the Lady* (1867) was the first novel written by Thomas Hardy (1840-1928). Karl Marx (1818-83) published *The Communist Manifesto* in 1848. James Joyce (1882-1941), one of the leading writers of the 20th century, wrote *Ulysses* in 1922, making a dull middle-aged man the protagonist of the story, and at the same time, he composed the story based on Homer's epic *Odysseia*…

Commanding a bird's-eye view of the history of humanitarianism, Wordsworth's foresight stands out. Because he was born in 1770, he was older than Gogol, Dostoevsky, Millet, and, of course, Dickens. Robert Southey (1774-1843) had written poems about the slave trade, the gothic world, and the poverty of the poor in 1797. Southey and Wordsworth were close friends, so Wordsworth may have been directly affected by Southey. Furthermore, although published posthumously, *The Prelude*, which is said to be Wordsworth's masterpiece, was an autobiographical epic in which the poet himself was set as the protagonist of the epic poem, and became a universal hero. Traditionally an epic poem was based on gods and kings. With *The Prelude*, it became decisive that Wordsworth was a groundbreaker. Wordsworth made an ordinary man into a hero who is as good as God. He also published *Poems, in Two Volumes* (1807), *The Excursion* (1814), *A Guide through the District of the Lakes* (1835), etc. Just as Walter Scott focused on the spirit of chivalry in medieval history, Wordsworth sought to revive the spirit of Christianity in nature and in the English countryside. Both of them were trying to show a way of life to those who had lost their humanity in a chaotic big city.

14. Austen and Dickens

In the Victorian period (1837-1901), not by the expression of poetry, but by the form of the novel, many writers sent a message to people. Now, the novel became the most effective way of expression. Walter Scott had already shifted from a poet to a historical novelist, and he became an international best-selling author. Before looking at Victorian writers, I would like to introduce Jane Austen (1775-1817) here, who is the first female novelist in England. She was born in a rectory in Hampshire, England. His father graduated from Oxford University and became a parish rector.

IT is a truth universally acknowledged, that a single man in possession of a good fortune, must be in want of a wife. However, little known the feelings or views of such a man may be on his first entering a neighbourhood, this truth is so well fixed in the minds of the surrounding families, that he is considered as the rightful property of some one or other of their daughters.[10]

Austen's masterpiece *Pride and Prejudice* (1813) begins with this sentence. The word *neighbourhood* is a British spelling, so it is not the American spelling *neighborhood*. Considering the content of the story, we think that Austen has just depicted ordinary and innocent events in everyday life with people in a middle-class family in the countryside of England at the end of the 18th century. Characters are conservative, not to make political or social statements, and don't say the slightest hint of social advancement of women. The author's argument is that a woman's happiness is to marry a rich and gentle person. But the universality of her novel is that all the characters are realistic and Austen is skillful at depicting the psychological description of young heroines. Austen said in one of her letters that if she has three or four families in a country village, she can write a novel. In any case, there is no doubt that Austen is the first female writer in British literature. She was not so famous when she was alive, and her fame came after her death. She died in Hampshire in 1817, at the age of 41.

Jane Austen

Then, the greatest Victorian novelist, Charles Dickens (1812-70) came out. Some of his brilliant works were *The Pickwick Papers* (1836-37), *Oliver Twist* (1837-38), *Christmas Carol* (1843), *David Copperfield* (1849-50), *A Tale of Two Cities* (1859), and *Great Expectations* (1860-61). Dickens himself had worked in a factory as a child, and worked as a clerk in law firms and courts before becoming a newspaper reporter. Many of the protagonists in his novels are orphans, poor, oppressed, and struggling boys, which reflect Dickens' own experiences. He excelled at vividly depicting the daily lives of middle- and lower-class people working in London. His works were just like a mirror, a reflection of the people living in the times. Literature was no longer for aristocrats, but

Charles Dickens

for the general people, and the English used became plain. The common people learned morality not from the Bible, but through novels. The following quote is from the opening paragraph of *The Mystery of Edwin Drood* (1870). It is interesting that Dickens adopted the detective story style in this last and unfinished novel of his.

An ancient English Cathedral town? How can the ancient English Cathedral town be here! The well-known massive grey square tower of its old Cathedral? How can that be here! There is no spike of rusty iron in the air, between the eye and it, from any point of the real prospect. What is the spike that intervenes, and who has set it up? Maybe, it is set up by the Sultan's orders for cymbals clash, and the Sultan goes by to his palace in long procession. Ten thousand scimitars flash in the sunlight, and thrice ten thousand dancing-girls strew flowers. Then, follow white elephants caparisoned in countless gorgeous colors, and infinite in number and attendants. Still, the Cathedral tower rises in the black-ground, where it cannot be, and still no writhing figure is on the grim spike. Stay! Is the spike so low a thing as the rusty spike on the top of a post of an old bedstead that has tumbled all awry? Some vague period of drowsy laughter must be devoted to the consideration of this possibility.[11]

After Dickens' novels, other important literary works appeared. Some of them are *Jane Eyre* (1847) by Charlotte Brontë, *Wuthering Heights* (1847) by Emily Brontë, *Silas Marner* (1861) by George Eliot (1819-80), *Alice's Adventures in Wonderland* (1865) by Lewis Carroll, *The Strange History of*

Charles Dickens Museum in London

Doctor Jekyll and Mister Hyde (1886) by Robert Louis Stevenson (1850-94), *Tess of the D'Urbervilles* (1891) by Thomas Hardy (1840-1928), *The Picture of Dorian Gray* (1891) by Oscar Wilde (1854-1900), *The Adventures of Sherlock Holmes* (1892) by Sir Arthur Conan Doyle (1859-1930), etc. Many masterpieces in the history of English literature were born during the Victorian era.

There is no doubt that *Alice*'s story had a great influence on the later film work of Japanese movie director Hayao Miyazaki (1941-), and it is no exaggeration to say that Carroll depicted a lively and active little girl for the first time in the history of English literature. Carroll was ahead of its time.

Hardy's *Tess*, which appears at the end of the Victorian era, is not an exemplary Victorian novel in which the protagonist grows up through experience, such as the forming novels of Dickens and George Eliot, but it's a tragic novel in which the protagonist dies an unjust death, showing a hopeless world that leaves the reader in despair. In the world where good perishes and evil flourishes, it is extremely important to make readers find meaning in life in despair and make them think more deeply about their life.

15. Charlotte Brontë

Charlotte Brontë was born in 1816, in Thornton, Yorkshire, England. She was the third of the six children (five daughters and a son). Because she was influenced by her age much younger than Jane Austen, and also because unlike Austen, she grew up in an unhappy family environment, Charlotte was not conservative and had a very radical personality. She portrayed strong-willed young girls, economically independent women, and women standing up to society in her novels. She was the eldest of three Brontë sisters: other two sisters are Ann Brontë (1820-49) whose masterpiece is *Agnes Grey*, and Emily Jane Brontë (1818-48) whose masterpiece is *Wuthering Heights*. Their father, Patrick Brontë, who became an Irish Anglican curate, born to a poor family in Northern Ireland, working very hard, and graduated from Cambridge University, was appointed the new rector for the village of Haworth in Yorkshire in 1820. The year after the Brontë family moved to Haworth, their mother Maria, who was small and weak, looked pale and tired, died at the age of 38.

Charlotte Brontë

When Charlotte was eight years old, four of her five daughters were sent to a boarding school, but due to unkind teachers, the cold, the poor food and bad hygiene, two sisters died from illness. Later, Charlotte went to school again to become a governess and in fact she became one. But she was disgusted by the poor working conditions of being used like a slave. She returned home and planned to open a private school with Emily at home. However, because the people of the town of Haworth were poor, not a single student came. Eventually, the three sisters began to write poetry and novels.

Charlotte's masterpiece, *Jane Eyre* (1847), is a powerful story about a young woman who seeks financial independence working as a governess (Charlotte herself had the same experience). In 1854, she married Irishman, Arthur Bell Nicholls, her father's curate, and soon became pregnant but suddenly died of a complication of pregnancy which causes excessive nausea and vomiting. That was just nine months after she got married. She was buried in the family vault in the Church of St Michael and All Angels at Haworth. Her age was only 38 years old. It was the same age as her mother, Maria died.

THERE was no possibility of taking a walk that day. We had been wandering, indeed, in the leafless shrubbery an hour in the morning; but since dinner (Mrs Reed, when there was no ceremony dined early) the cold winter wind had brought with it clouds so sombre, and a rain so penetrating, that further outdoor exercise was now out of the question.[12]

The quote is from the beginning of *Jane Eyre*. The absence of a period in *Mrs* and the fact that *sombre* is not spelled *somber* are characteristics of British English. The book was originally published under the male name *Currer Bell*. The initials of the pen-name C.B. are the same initials as her name Charlotte Brontë. *Jane Eyre* is a story about a

Queen Victoria

rebellious orphan girl with a sense of gender equality, who grows up and eventually falls in love with Mr. Rochester, the owner of the manor house where she lives as a governess. On the day of the wedding, Mrs. Rochester, who had lost her sanity and had been confined to the old tower of the manor house for many years, suddenly appears (her existence in revealed), and such grotesque atmosphere and background also suggest Gothic tastes that were popular in the Victorian era. Brontë shows the world a love marriage that is not bound by social status. She also shows a new image of a woman, who is strong, intelligent, and independent. Jane is a woman who can control her own life. Her way of life aroused a great response at the time. The spirit of the heroine, Jane, is effective enough for the girls of the world living in the 21st century now, and it will be a great message for women of all generations.

Afternoon Tea served at Rihga Royal Hotel Tokyo

16. Conan Doyle and Detective Stories

Many Victorian writers wrote for newspapers and magazines at first, and some of them were also editors. When the serialized work in the magazine was completed, they put them together and published a book. Magazines and books were established as products for the general public. Society was changing. The middle class became very powerful, and writers educated businesslike people in those days. Novelists entertained people, and at the same time they played the role of making people think deeply about life. The Victorian era was the heyday of the novel. The following quote is from the opening part of 'The Speckled Band' (1892) by Arthur Conan Doyle.

In glancing over my notes of the seventy odd cases in which I have during the last eight years studied the methods of my friend Sherlock Holmes, I find many tragic, some comic, a large number merely strange, but none commonplace; for working as he did rather for the love of his art than for the acquirement of wealth, he refused to associate himself with any investigation which did not tend towards the unusual, and even the fantastic.[13]

Sir Arthur Conan Doyle

'The Speckled Band' is a short story published in *The Strand Magazine* (1891-1950), a monthly English magazine for the general public to enjoy reading with their family members. Sherlock Holmes series consists of 56 short stories and four long stories, for a total of 60 works (1887-1927). The name of *Sherlock* has an image of Shylock, a Jewish moneylender of Shakespeare's *The Merchant of Venice*, then *Sherlock Holmes* also sounds like 'She locks Holmes' or 'Sure, lock homes.' Of course, Conan Doyle was a pioneer of detective stories and subsequently, his works became classic, and they are still very popular all over the world. However, what is noteworthy about Doyle's Holmes stories is that there are many international characters in every story. Dr. Watson, the best friend of Holmes, was a disabled veteran military doctor from Afghanistan. The names of Watson and Mrs. Hudson who lived downstairs and cared for Holmes and Watson, suggest their ancestors came from the Scandinavian Peninsula because of their family names ending in -*son*. King of Bohemia in 'A Scandal in Bohemia' (1891) is the main character of the story, and his former mistress, Irene Adler was born in New Jersey, America, who became an opera singer in Warsaw, Poland. In 'The Boscombe Valley Mystery' (1891), most of the characters involved in the incident were from Australia. In 'The Man with the Twisted Lip' (1891), there is a Chinese villain who runs an opium house in London. Dr. Roylott in 'The Speckled Band' (1892), who killed his step-daughter was once a doctor in India. Henry Wood, a tragic hero in 'The Crooked Man' (1893), was a brave soldier in India. In 'The Greek Interpreter' (1893), main characters were all Greeks. In 'The Final Problem' (1893), Holmes was commissioned by the French government to solve a serious incident, and he last confronted Professor Moriarty at the Swiss waterfall, called the Reichenbach Falls. In 'The Dancing Men' (1903), Elsie, the heroin in trouble came from America to get married to an English gentleman, who was killed by her former American lover. In 'The Six Napoleons' (1904), criminals including Beppo are

Inside the Sherlock Holmes Museum in London

all Italians. In 'The Abbey Grange' (1904), Lady Mary Brackenstall is a young beautiful woman from Australia. In 'Wisteria Lodge' (1908), there are many Spaniards appearing throughout the whole story. In 'The Problem of Thor Bridge' (1922), the main character in the story is an American, and his wife was a Brazilian who had killed herself. The stories of Sherlock Holmes are full of international flair. The Victorian British Empire had many colonies and its territory spread all over the world. In the 19th century, the English had already acquired a global sense, and it will take more than 100 years for a country to become a truly international nation.

17. Class Society and Sexuality

D. H. Lawrence (David Herbert Richards Lawrence) was born in Nottinghamshire, England, in 1885, as the third son (fourth child) of a father (a coal miner) and a mother (a former pupil-teacher). He grew up in a working-class family. After graduating from University of Nottingham, he worked as an elementary school teacher before becoming a writer. He lived in Germany for two years from 1912 and married a German woman after returning to England. One of his best works, *Sons and Lovers* (1913), is said to be his autobiographical novel. It is a novel that clearly shows that Lawrence himself grew up strongly influenced by his mother. Of course, the meaning of the title is that for a mother whose love for her husband has cooled down, her sons are really lovers. He went to Australia and Mexico, and spent two years in the United States from September 1922, writing *Studies in Classic American Literature*. In 1926, he lived in Florence, Italy, and wrote his last novel, *Lady Chatterley's Lover* (published privately in 1928, in Italy and America, and in 1929, in France), which

D. H. Lawrence

made a large sum of money. However, by this time he had already contracted tuberculosis and had only a short life expectancy. He then moved to Vence, France, where he died at the age of 44, in 1930. Many of his works boldly depict men's and women's roles in sexual relationships and the theme of human sex and love. *The Rainbow* (1915) and *Women in Love* (1920) were banned on publication in the UK for being obscene. *Lady*

The house where Lawrence lived and the plaque showing it

Chatterley's Lover was also banned until 1960. In Japan, there was the *Lady Chatterley* trial, in which Sei ITO's translation was accused of being obscene.

> OURS IS ESSENTIALLY a tragic age, so we refuse to take it tragically. The cataclysm has happened, we are   among the ruins, we start to build up new little habits, to have new little hopes. It is rather hard work: there is now no smooth road into the future: but we go round, or scramble over the obstacles. We've got to live, no matter how many skies have fallen. This was more or less Constance Chatterley's position. The war had brought the roof down over her head. And she had realised that one must live and learn. She married Clifford Chatterley in 1917, when he was home for a month on leave...[14]

This quote is the opening part of *Lady Chatterley's Lover*. It is clear that this story is not just about a romance of an upper-class woman, the wife of an aristocrat who repeatedly had an affair with the gamekeeper Oliver Mellors who came from a working-class background, but a story that sharply criticized the British class system at the time and also criticized modern civilization. The view that the age we live in is fundamentally tragic would also lead to Wordsworth's "sad music of humanity." Also, we shouldn't miss the word "realised" which is not spelled "realized" because it's the British spelling.

Just as Wordsworth sought human recovery through nature and Scott through medieval chivalry, Lawrence sought to escape the stresses of modern society through sexual liberation. I think his obsession with sexual issues was due not only to the reaction to the sexual oppression of the Victorian era, but also to the influence of the psychologist and psychoanalyst Freud (1856-1939) . For a deeper understanding of literary works, correct knowledge of philosophy, religion, and psychology would be essential.

Because many famous politicians, artists, writers, inventors and scholars from home and abroad lived in London, there are many circular Blue Plaques on the exterior of the buildings, small explanatory plaques indicating the houses in which the remarkable individuals once lived. It is casually attached to the wall of the building so as not to destroy the cityscape and not to cause trouble to the people who currently live there. For tourists, searching around London with maps and guidebooks is as fun as a treasure hunt. Although D. H. Lawrence spent most of his life abroad, he also lived in London in 1915. The address where he lived is 1 Byron Villas, Vale of Heath, Hampstead, NW3. Now a blue plaque is on the wall of the red brick house.

18. Cockney

As regards Cockney, it is one of the typical English dialects that has spread in the East End, London. It was the language that was spoken by working-class people living in the East End since the early 19th century. The etymology of Cockney originally refers to a poorly shaped egg that looks like it was born by a rooster, or a cock. In the Middle Ages, it was a term that meant a soft and spoiled boy who grew up in the City. Later, at the end of the 15th century, it referred to those who were born within hearing of the bells of the church of St Mary-le-Bow in the City. In the 17th century, it referred to the common people who lived in London for generations. In the 18th and 19th centuries, after the Industrial Revolution, workers flocked to London, especially into the East End, so the word, Cockney, came to refer to these uneducated workers.

Their way of pronunciation was very unique and sometimes difficult to understand: *I don't know* would be "I donno." Sometimes, *isn't it?* would be pronounced and written as "innit?". They pronounce *a* [ei] as [ai]: for example, *able* is pronounced as [aibi], *day* is as [dai], and *plate* is [plait]. And *th* is pronounced as [f] or [v]: *theatre* is as "featre", *think* is as "fink", and *that* is as "vat", *with* is as "wiv". Also, they don't pronounce *h* sound in a word. For example, *half* is pronounced as [a:f], *house* is as [æus], *has* is [az] and *he* is [i:]. If the indefinite article is added, they pronounce *a* as "an": for example, *a hand* is like [ənænd]. Cockney English does not pronounce [h], but on the contrary, some people are too concerned that they sometimes make an effort to add [h] sound when they don't need to pronounce it. For example, *ever* is [hevə]. Also, between vowels, there may be a non-existent [r] sound: for example, *America is* is pronounced like "America ris".

Cockney English also has many hidden expressions. They prefer expressions that could only be understood among them. For example, *Adam and Eve* means "believe". *Could you Adam and Eve it?* means "Could you believe it?". What's interesting is that *Eve* and (beli)*eve* rhyme each other. In general, there are many hidden nouns in Cockney, and they rhyme with endings. For example, *Bread and Honey* means Mo*ney*, *Donkey's Ears* means Y*ears*, *Lady Godiva* means Fi*ver* (5 pound note), *Pony* means 25 *poun*ds, *Tea leaf* stands for Thi*ef*.

And as the Irish people can say, *my* in the sentence can be said, "me." This is also Cockney English. For example, *me heart* can be "my heart" and *meself* is "myself". Short forms of "am not," "are not," "is not," "have not," and "has not" will all be *ain't*. As for *ain't*, which often appears in Irish English or Black English in America, it first appeared in London, in 1706. It was used in the sense of "am not" in the early 19th century, and it came to be used in the meaning of "aren't" and "isn't" in the Cockney dialect of London.

Audrey Hepburn during the filming of the movie *My Fair Lady* in 1964

Irish great writer, George Bernard Shaw (1856-1950) wrote a drama called *Pygmalion* in 1913, which is known as a musical, titled *My Fair Lady*.

In 1964, a musical of the same name was decided to make a film and produced in the United States. The movie starring Audrey Hepburn (1929-93) became her biggest hit. It won the Academy Award for Best Picture in the same year, including other eight awards, and was also a big hit in Japan. The story is about a flower girl in London named Eliza Doolittle, who speaks Cockney English, learns to speak proper English (RP: Received Pronunciation) through Mr. Henry Higgins, who is a linguistics and phonetics specialist. Eliza, after all, masters upper-class English. Professor Higgins didn't treat her as a human at first, but gradually finds himself attracted to her. On the other hand, Eliza learns Queen's English and at the same time begins to gain confidence in herself and acquire a strong self. In the original, *Pygmalion*, Prof. Henry Higgins has a broken heart at the end of the story, but in the musical, it is a happy ending that suggests the two become a couple. This movie is a treasure trove of Cockney English and it is an extremely informative and valuable work.

Today, many young Londoners think it's cool to speak Cockney, and people who are not working-class and don't live in the East End tend to speak Cockney. Perhaps one of the reasons for this phenomenon is that a great star football player like David Beckham ((1975-) also speaks Cockney. Beckham, who once dominated the world was born in London. He was known as a footballer prodigy from a young age.

Beckham went on to play regularly for Manchester United and became captain of the England national team. He later moved to Los Angeles Galaxy in the USA. Beckham was also known to speak Cockney in interviews, but lately he tried to fix Cockney. If you compare the old interviews with the current interviews, the English he speaks today is quite standard American English.

19. Scottish English

Most Scottish people originally spoke Celtic (Scottish Gaelic). During the reign of Malcolm III (1031-93) Gaelic ended its role as an official language of Scotland. However, it continued to be used in the Scottish Highlands until the 16th century and then declined. Also, there is a language called Scots language, which belongs to the Germanic language, originated in Old English. It was used mainly in the Lowlands. Scottish poet, Robert Burns (1759-96) wrote the poem "Auld Lang Syne" (Old Long Since) in the Scots language. Sir Walter Scott (1771-1832) also used the language in the conversation part of his historical novels. Sir James M. Barrie (1860-1937), the author of the drama *Peter Pan*, used the Scots language in his works as well.

The Scottish Standard English appeared after the 17th century. This is undoubtedly due to the fact that King James VI of Scotland became King James I of England in 1603. This fact brought a closer relationship between Scotland and England. And then the Acts of Union 1707 made two kingdoms become one by the name of the Kingdom of Great Britain (including Wales).

Should auld acquaintance be forgot,

And never brought to mind?

Should auld acquaintance be forgot,

And auld lang syne?

For auld lang syne, my jo,

For auld lang syne,

Scottish hero Robert the Bruce   Glamis Castle, a typical Scottish tower house

We'll tak' a cup o'kindness yet,

For auld lang syne.

And surely ye'll be your pint-stoup!

And surely, I'll be mine!

And we'll tak' a cup of kindness yet,

For auld lang syne.

Excerpt from "Auld Lang Syne"

In Scotland, the words such as *Mac*, *Mc*, *M'* are sometimes prefixed to surnames. Their meaning is *son of* or *descendant of*. Examples include MacArthur, Macbeth, MacGregor, MacKenzie, MacLean, MacMillan, and McDonald. They were originally used in the families of nobles and large landowners, but later came to be used by ordinary people as well. From around the 12th century, they came to be used as one of the ordinary surnames. Irish people also use a surname with the Mac. In Ireland, *O'* is often used in the sense of *son of*. For example, O'Hara, O'Neil,

Molrose Abbey, Scottish Borders

O'Neill, O'Neal, etc. *Fitz-* is a Norman expression meaning *son of*, but originally it came from Latin *filius* (=son). *Fitzgerald* (*FitzGerald*) was particularly used by Irish aristocratic families. There are also surnames with *-son*, as used in northern England, to mean *son* or *descendant*. These include Anderson, Donaldson, Dickson, Gibson, Henderson, Morrison, Robertson, Stevenson, Simpson, Watson, and Wilson.

The name *Scott* originally means *Scot*, or *Scottish*. Some of the Scots who had lived in Ireland settled in present-day Scotland in the 6th century, resulting in the country being called "Scotland" because it was the land where the Scots lived. English people called the Scottish people *Scot (t)*; hence, the surname *Scott* appeared. The surname *Jones* is also common in Scotland, and the *-s* ending is thought to mean Jone's son. Tony Blair, who served as Prime Minister of the United Kingdom from 1997 to 2007, was born in Edinburgh. *Blair* is one of the names of popular place names in Scotland. It means *flat land*. Other typical place names used are: *Aber* (estuary), *Dun* (hill, fort), *Eilean* (Island), *Glen* (valley), and *Loch* (lake).

20. David Hume

An indispensable element in the history of Western philosophy is the British Empiricism. The philosopher who perfected this idea at the opposite position of the Continental Rationalism was David Hume from Scotland. Mentioning Hume, the greatest philosopher born in Britain, is essential to the history of Scotland.

David Hume (1711-76) was born in Edinburgh, the capital of Scotland, as the second son of Joseph Home (Hume), a lawyer and the 10th branch of the Earl of Home family. He lost his father when he was two years old. He entered the University of Edinburgh at the age of 11 to study law, but dropped out. Later, living at his family home in Berwickshire, Scotland, he immersed himself in philosophical studies. Although Hume himself did not profess to be an atheist, he missed out on professorships at the University of Edinburgh and the University of Glasgow because he was considered an atheist. He served as a tutor to the children of nobles, military aide-de-camp, librarian (at the University of Edinburgh), and later held positions such as secretary to the French ambassador, British Chargé d'affaires, and Under Secretary of State for Northern Department. He criticized Descartes, and he was the first philosopher to have skepticism about God. He also denied innate ideas. He was a hardcore skeptic and an atheist. He was an opinion leader of Britain's empiricists, along with Bacon (1561-1626) and

David Hume

Locke (1632-1704), and it can be said that British empiricism was perfected by him.

Descartes' "Cogito Ergo Sum" (I think, therefore I am) made epistemology the central problem of modern philosophy, and from then on, rational theory became mainstream. But modern philosophy later divided into two groups. One is the continental rationalism begun with Descartes, which regards reason as absolute, later divided into German idealism and French materialism. The other is English empiricism that emphasizes experience while acknowledging human imperfections with Hume as the perfector. The former is a method of drawing a conclusion according to a certain logical or mathematical rule, such as, if "A = B" and "B = C", then "A = C", or a method of drawing another new conclusion starting from some premise (deduction). The latter is a method of finding common concepts from many observations and drawing provisional conclusions (induction).

Empiricism is the position that correct knowledge can be obtained from information, that is, experience, which has originally entered through the five human senses. The founder of empiricism was the English philosopher Bacon, born in 1561 before Descartes, and he valued experience more than logical thinking such as rational theory. Bacon's thought was succeeded by subsequent generations, an English philosopher John Locke, an Irish philosopher George Berkeley (1685-1753), and David Hume, the Scotsman. Locke argued that the mind at birth is like a blank slate *tabula rasa* with no knowledge, and that our knowledge comes from observation and experience. Locke denied the existence of innate ideas. Locke's empiricism was closer to idealism in terms of methodological attitudes because it sought to show the structure of recognition through the exploration of the ideas that consciousness creates on the basis of experience. Hume's thought also inherits this attitude of Locke. But Hume strongly criticized metaphysics.

Berkeley explained that to exist is to be perceived. In other words, everything in this world can be perceived not because it exists, but because it is perceived, it can exist. He denied the existence of material substance, and insisted that familiar objects like books and pencils are ideas perceived by the human mind and cannot exist without being perceived. Everything around us, clothes, food, buildings, plants, rivers, mountains, the sun, the moon, etc., does not exist independently there. Existence refers to the perception by which someone sees or hears anything. He also argued that there is no such thing as something that is not perceived by all human beings in the world, but rather that it exists because God perceives it. This is an idea that has become extreme because of the emphasis on experience. Then Hume came along, insisting that the mind itself is simply "a bundle of perceptions". In other words, there is not even the human mind that Berkeley admitted. Hume believed that there was no substance in the world, but only perception. He argued that the human mind, as well as Descartes' self in "Cogito Ergo Sum," consists of nothing more than a bundle of knowledge and perception received from experience, and has no substance.

Hume held that passions rather than reason govern human behavior. Hume argued that we experience only a bundle of sensations, and the self is nothing more than this bundle of causally-connected perceptions. The philosopher who said, "Man is a bundle of perceptions," insisted that perception (all that appears in the mind) is divided into two: impressions and ideas. And he thought all ideas were born from impressions, and impressions were the cause and ideas were the result. There are simple and complex respectively. The human mind is made up of overlapping experiences, and that knowledge is formed by the combined ideas.

Hume remained skeptical of trust in reason. He held that concepts that do not exist in reality, that is, the products of the imagination, are all combinations of past experiences. Expectancy of the future is just based on past experience. Hume considered even God to be a concept created from a combination of multiple experiences.

According to Hume, it is only by experience that one object can be inferred from one object to another. For example, "when approaching the flame, it is hot" is not caused by the temperature of the flame, but the experience of "approaching the fire" and feeling "it is hot" occurs one after another, and when it overlaps, people expect heat just by looking at the flame. In other words, causality means that one is perceived or remembered, and the other is supplemented to coincide with past experiences.

Hume's thought follows theory of ideas in epistemology and belongs to the lineage of idealism that follows a German philosopher, Georg Wilhelm Friedrich Hegel (1770-1831). Hume was opposed to materialism. After all, Hume's philosophy influenced not only analytic philosophy which has been the mainstream in the English-speaking world since the 20th century, but also continental philosophy which has been the mainstream since the 19th century, especially a German philosopher, Immanuel Kant (1724-1804).

Hume published a number of books, including *The Treatise of Human Nature* (1739-1740), *Political discourses* (1752), and *The History of England* (1755-1762). He died in Edinburgh at the age of 65 from abdominal cancer. He remained atheist throughout his life.

21. Sir Walter Scott

Scott (1771-1832) is the greatest Scottish novelist. Two years before Scott's birth, James Watt (1736-1819) built the first efficient steam engine, which was probably the most important invention of the Industrial Revolution. In the year when Scott was born, Richard Arkwright (1732-92) invented the water frame spinning machine, which could save a lot of labor. Since then, many factories had been built in the north of England and in the Midlands. This is the age of the Industrial Revolution in the 18th century that had altered the appearance of the country as well as the ways people lived in and worked. Machines became almighty, and human beings were paid little attention, regarded as mere subsidiary labor. Women or little boys had to drag the coal along the dark and small tunnels. Rationalization of industry being pushed ahead with, utilitarianism was systematized and developed by Jeremy Bentham (1748-1832) who is considered as the "Father of Utilitarianism", and John Stuart Mill (1806-73) who was an

advocate for Bentham. Against this stream of the history, the stream of natural science and technology becoming the main current, a large number of philosophers, theologians, or men of letters rang alarms continuously. With trial and error, they had intended to set a matter in the right direction in many ways. This tendency still went on during the 19th century and even in the end of the 20th century as is generally known.

Sir Walter Scott

In Britain, the 18th century was, as it were, a

savage and dangerous age, despite the extreme economic prosperity. In these difficult situations, some people came to feel nostalgia for the past. The life style and social system of the past, especially the medieval times, became an example of life. Chivalry was again accepted as a model in the confused society. In the Middle Ages, religious people believed in many miracles of God, having fertile imagination, and myths or legends were richly in close contact with them. Kings and feudal lords looked after the poor just like their parents, wherefore all classes were linked together. The lower class was under the protection of the upper class, or the ruling class, whereon medieval Catholic churches gave the wealth of the rich to the poor. They thought that the Middle Ages were full of love and philanthropy, tolerance and generosity.

Some came to think that people in the Middle Ages had been much happier than contemporaries of them; others thought that they should recur to their former Ages, which might stop the collapse of the society. For them, the restoration of medievalism was the best way to clear the contradiction so that they could maintain public order. Meanwhile, Britain as a nation grew up larger and became much stronger. Union of England and Ireland in 1800, victory of the battle of Trafalgar in 1805, and winning of the Napoleonic Wars (1800-15) after

the battle of Waterloo raised patriotic spirit of the British people. With their economic success, the country grew up one of the top-ranking nations in Europe, which let them feel nationalism. This is the time when British people would look back to the Celtic cultures

Abbotsford, a country houes built by Walter Scott

and the history of the Anglo-Saxons

they had never appreciated before because of their crudeness. The old romance such as King Arthur's seems to have been very popular in those days.

The reason why Celtic or Germanic races' cultures received much attention or why medievalism was suddenly popular among the people was that being different from the 18th century classicism idealizing and imitating of the Greek and Roman civilization and literature; they yearned after their own original cultures which were unsophisticated but never untouched by foreign cultures. It was James Macpherson (1736-96) who published *Ossianic Poems*. Thomas Percy (1729-1811) also published *Reliques of Ancient English Poetry* in 1765. At the same year, Horace Walepole (1717-97) wrote a Gothic novel *The Castle of Otranto*. It is clear that their works had a strong influence on the popularity of the medievalism subsequently.

In any case, returning to the past or former state, some people tried to have vivid medieval experience in order to spread the range of vision to judge the unknown society controlled over by machinery or by other unknown powers. They came to think that medieval knights were heroes who were primitive, brilliant nature lovers, broad-minded, and creative. They thought that medieval people should be praised, and words, such as "Gothic" or "grotesque", which only had negative meanings before, now came to have an affirmative meaning. Although buried themselves in obscurity until then, ancient times' legendary and ballads were suddenly received recognition, and were made much of. It was in this time that Walter Scott published *The Minstrelsy of the Scottish Border* (1802), and such important works as *The Lay of the Last Minstrel* (1805), *Marmion* (1808), and *The Lady of the Lake* (1810). At that time, Scott devoted himself exclusively to the past of Scotland. Scott regarded himself as a minstrel of his age and left many of his works. Then attained celebrity as an epic poet, his works were accepted by a large number of people in his age.

Afterwards, he became a historical novelist, and wrote twenty-seven historical novels. Scott was sometimes said to be a medievalist, and actually he found many themes in the medieval Scotland and reconstructed its world. However, at the same time, he knew the boundaries of it. He knew the uncivilized aspect of its world. Scott did not seem to wish for the past to come back. The idea that Scott really wanted to say is not the same as the current ones, but something else.

Scotland was a country which had once collapsed, but it merged into Britain well. It was the progress of history. What is in the base of Scott's works is that Scott always tried to find some kind of order in Scotland. In the long term of history, he sought for the missing piece of Scottish history. He tried to find the generosity and elegance in the Scottish characters, which had been regarded as violence and roughness. One must be aware of the violent and chaotic history that Scotland had. Before reading Scott's works, one can never evaluate the true meanings of his works. Scott always wished the better behavior of the people. Law and order were pressing needs for Scotland. He was not anti-establishment, Considering the barbarian history of Scotland, Scott was totally a gradualist. In this sense, he was a reformist and not an anachronism. This kind of personality was necessary for Scotland at that time. Scott played an important role in Scottish history. He influenced many Scottish people who felt nostalgia for their lost homeland. Scott admitted the reality and tried to cultivate Scotland. He did not seek for the new values, but he tried to grow the society as they were. If one studies the history of Scotland, one will never think of revolutionizing Scottish society. Scotland was always too chaotic and unstable to be a developed country. And it collapsed. Independence lost.

Some people said Scott was too submissive to the English government. He was too wholesome. Sometimes, as a writer, Scott was criticized for it. But his wholesomeness was what Scotland really needed at that time. That brought King George IV to Scotland in 1822, and made Queen Victoria one of Scott fans, who favored Highlanders and built Balmoral Castle in Scottish baronial style in 1853. Scott contributed a lot to improve the image of Scotland, especially brave Highlanders. He appealed to the world that Scotland had its own romance, which raised it up to art. That made people understand what they had never tried to know. There we can find Scott's attitude to include all different ideas to unite. All the introductory epistles of *Marmion* are pipelines between fiction and non-fiction. Also, to list many historical facts made people realize that history is alive and still going on. Chivalry in romances meant the spirit of loving adventures and kindness to ladies. A knight was supposed to be brave, virtuous,

Abbotsford is now open to the public

and a devoted Christian. Scott's sense for the medieval had two sides. On the one hand, as nostalgic people and the medieval lovers say, Scott thought that a society based on chivalry was better than a society based on commercialism. On the other hand, Scott knew the uncivilized aspect of the Age of Chivalry, and he did not seem to wish for the Medieval to come back as the medievalists wanted to. Scott did not criticize the modern society by making the medieval a model. Scott affirmed the sympathy and generosity of the knight but he denied the attitude of chivalry only focused on fame. Scott found his themes mostly in the Medieval and reconstructed its world, but at the same time he learned the bounds of it. Scott was often attracted by the heroic acts of brave Scottish soldiers. Scott instinctively felt that the medieval society had immeasurable power hidden, which would give its strong-hold of life to modern fragile daily life. Scott commanded his creativity in analyzing the medieval world suffering with an evil chivalry. In one sense, Scott was a realist and he had a keen sensitivity to the society and times. He had a desire to describe an idealistic world and characters that fit to the 19th century. He did not seek for the ideal in the Middle Ages. He just borrowed themes from the medieval romances to seek how he could save Scottish spirits in the 19th century. While he stuck to the past, Scott also believed in the progress of the society. His father was a lawyer and Scott also became a lawyer in the court. What he hated most was a disorder or chaos. To develop an idealistic society, he thought it was necessary to have legal procedures. It was Scott's will that in *The Lady* Ellen did not prefer to be radical, so that she refused to marry Roderick, chieftain of the Highlands. Scott did not like an extreme violence and he denied people who were extremely barbaric. We would like to look into what the age of Douglas tells us. Douglas, one of the main characters in *The Lady* is an old exiled knight, yet he is close to saint. When he was young, he might have been a model of chivalry: the spirit of loving quests for fame, single-fights, the spirit that feels an honorable death is beautiful, etc. He might have had a painful separation with his love. He might have lost his mind in his own bravery like Roderick, which was the reason why King James got suspicions with and exiled him. Scott created an ideal knight called Douglas past middle age, who went through hardship. King James is in his middle age, but he does not seem as a knight of caliber as Douglas. King James is a likable hero, who has an affair with a lady of the lake, and loves adventures. However, he does not quite seem to acquire the true chivalry yet. Moreover, not as an individual's level, but if we have a bird eye, we could overlap our lives with history. Scott tried to influence both England and Scotland with Douglas' spirit. He wished to mingle Scotland and England together, and to have all struggles end. He wished for the mature and stable society. Scott tried to realize in his works for Scottish society to merge into English-like. Scott created a fictional knight Douglas who was matured years in order to make chivalry suitable for the modern society. This matured chivalry is based on "twilight" and "sympathy", and it shows Scott's sense of beauty towards harmony. Here, the sense of harmony and Douglas' spirit (chivalry) are almost the same. With this sense, Scott quietly observed the history of Scottish, English, and Irish races to integrate.

Many memorable words in Scottish history are used very often in *Marmion*. Scott might have thought that he must leave Scottish history in some way or other. Scott regarded himself as a minstrel of his age and left his works. These are the reasons why he stuck to the things that had changed or vanished, and also times, places, and proper nouns were very important factors for his works. Scott passionately restored the Medieval in the period of enlightenment in Scotland. Equally important, Scott contributed Scotland to recover its status.

The Lowlands were on English side, and Scott, one of Lowlanders, was basically on English side. Yet, he also had feelings towards Highlanders. He wanted to find romanticism in them. According to the modern history of Britain, many Highland soldiers died in the war when the British Empire extended its colonies. Many Highlanders were sent to new colonies overseas; others lost their lands when the Highland Clearances were put into operation. In spite of these cruel treatment from British government, Highlanders never lost their honor and pride. As it were, what stopped riots to break out in Scotland might have been due to Scott's works. In *Waverley* (1814), Scott says:

> These reveries he was permitted to enjoy, undisturbed by queries or interruption; and it was in many a winter walk by the shores of Ulswater, that he acquired a more complete mastery of a spirit tamed by adversity, than his former experience had given him; and that he felt himself entitled to say firmly, though perhaps with a sigh, that the romance of his life was ended, and that its real history had now commenced.[15]

This quote can be interpreted as his message for Scotland, Land of his sires, that medieval Scotland had ended. Scott showed the glorious past of Scotland to encourage Scottish people to take pride in them. However, one should not stick to one's past. What Scott meant in this part is to make progress by facing reality, which is firmly based on history. History is the gradual change of time towards harmony, and that although the paths are full of trials and tribulations, it is so fair with a sense of Christianity.

22. Irish English

The Act of Union 1800 had made Ireland part of the United Kingdom. At present, Ireland consists of Northern Ireland of the UK and the Republic of Ireland in the south. Before that, many Scottish people living in the Lowlands landed on the northern part of the isle and settled there. Therefore, Northern Ireland's English was said to be close to Scottish English.

Since the 5th century B.C., Irish (Gaelic) was being used as a native language. In the 12th century, Old English came in temporarily with Anglo-Norman knights, but not like the Scots language, it never developed into the Irish language. In the 16th century, King Henry VIII of England became the king of Ireland. As a result of the Tudor monarchs' invasion and colonization, the use of Irish was banned and English was brought to Ireland. English became dominant in the urban area in the 18th century, and in the next century, English was also used in rural areas. Finally, English was used everywhere in Ireland. After independence, the revival of the Irish language was promoted, but Irish English was firmly established. The characteristics of Irish English at that time were as follows. "I am not" or "I'm not" were replaced as "I amn't." The Irish tended to speak fast, and they rarely used "Yes" or "No" when they answered. For example, if they were asked "Do you like to sing songs?" they would say, "I do." John Millington Synge (1871-1909), the most important playwright of Ireland never used "Yes" or "No" in his plays. Instead, he used Irish regional language

Dublin, capital of Ireland

George Bernard Shaw

and settings.

The Irishman George Bernard Shaw (1856-1950) was one of the greatest playwrights in the 20th century English drama. Among his works, *Pygmalion* (1913), which is known as a musical or movie, titled *My Fair Lady,* is definitely his representative work. He wrote 53 satire-filled plays in his life. He did not believe in Christianity, and he made political remarks actively. He described a variety of people, including common people full of energy and courage, cynically, and humorously, such as a professor and a flower-selling girl. In 1925, Shaw received the Nobel Prize in Literature, subject to donation of prize money. In his later years, he was proposed to be given the title of Knight by the British Royal Family, but refused to do so. We can find a lot of Irish English expressions in his first successful play, *John Bull's Other Island* in 1904.

Tim. A salary, is it? Sure I'd do it for nothin, only me cloes ud disgrace you; and I'd be dhriven to borra money from your friends: a thing that's agin me nacher. But I won't take a penny more than a hundred a year.

Broadbent. If that will satisfy you —

Tim. Why shouldn't it satisfy me? A hundred a year is twelve-pound a month, isn't it?

Broadbent. No. Eight pound six and eightpence.

Tim. Oh murder! An I'll have to sind five timme poor oul mother in Ireland[16]

James Joyce (1882-1941) born and educated in Ireland was the greatest novelist in the 20th century English literature. All the stages of his novels were in Ireland. He became famous for using a new writing style, known as "a stream of consciousness," which greatly influenced on the later writers. *Dubliners* (1914), *A Portrait of an Artist as a Young Man* (1916), *Ulysses* (1922), and *Finnegan's Wake* (1939) are his masterpieces. The following quote is from the impressive ending part of *Ulysses.*

> …O that awful deepdown torrent O and the sea the sea crimson sometimes like fire and the glorious sunsets and figtrees in the Almeda gardens yes and all the queer little streets and pink and blue and yellow houses and the rosegardens and the jessamine and geraniums and cactuses and Gibraltar as a girl where I was a Flower of the mountain yes when I put the rose in my hair like the Andalusian girls used or shall I wear a red yes and how he kissed me under the Moorish wall and I thought well as well him as another and then I asked him with my eyes to ask again yes and then he asked me would I yes to say yes my mountain flower and first I my arms around him yes and drew him down to me so he could feel my breasts all perfume yes and his heart was going like mad and yes I said yes I will Yes.[17]

The novel title *Ulysses* is the English version of Latin *Ulysseus* or *Ulixes* who is a Greek mythological hero, Odysseus (Odyssey), and consisting of more than 680 pages in paperback. The novel written by Joyce is a work composed of 18 episodes that depict the undistinguished events of a day in Dublin, Ireland, and are full of thoughts and feelings of the ordinary characters. However, they are representatives of heroes in Homer's epic, *Odyssea* in the 8th century BC, and it links them to cross ancient and modern history. The daily life of middle-aged unpopular Dubliners is depicted using esoteric terms, and sometimes the characters' monologues continue endlessly. The main settings of the story are as follows: the parapet of the tower, school, Sandymount strand, Eccles Street, All Hallows (church), Westland row, a pharmacy, the mosque of the baths, Prospects (graveyard), a lane of sepulchers, the Press, the national library, the Ormond (hotel) bar, Barney Kiernan's (inn), hospital, whore town, the cabman's shelter (tearoom), and the bedroom. In the ninth episode, the philosophers Plato, Aristotle, later Socrates appeared, and Shakespeare is called "Saxon Shakespeare," then the author introduces the theory that Shakespeare had a son named "Hamnet Shakespeare" who died at the age of 20. *Hamlet* is said to be a tragic work created in the image of his dead son. His masterpiece was greatly influenced by his own life. There are various words in the text: musical terms such as piano, diminuendo, a tempo, stringendo; Latin, Italian, French, German, Gaelic; frequently quotes from Shakespeare plays and sonnets. In the fourteenth episode, there are many topics about obstetrics, gynecology, mother's womb, pregnancy, fetus, and childbirth, expressed in various writing ways using old English-style, Middle English-style, Latin, Irish, etc. The final eighteenth episode is tremendous; its original title was "Penelope," the name of Odyssey's chaste wife. The content of the text is only the image of the cheating wife of Leopold Bloom in bed. It is exclusively her inner monologue, in other words, "the stream of consciousness" that covers more than 40 pages without apostrophes or commas, and almost no punctuation marks. It should be noted that in the distant past, the person who should be the main character of the story was God, the royalty and aristocracy, the hero, the great man, and the ideal person. More than 2,000 years later, they became strange literary young men or ordinary middle-aged people who could not be models, and who could not be the main characters of the story before. A mixture of traditional Catholic worldviews and metaphors of obscene sexual depictions is also a feature of this work. The experimental novel was published in Paris in 1922. It was four years after the end of the First World War (1914-1918), by which more than 16 million people were killed. As the quote above, this chaotic and avant-garde novel ends with the word, "Yes." This is indeed symbolic and it is a sign of Joyce's hope for the future of humanity. This literary work is undoubtedly one of the goals of world literature in the 20th century.

James Joyce

Literary works are the best sample of the language of the country. The writing style and the words used at that time are reflections of its national characters and represent a manifestation of the language progress. If the work written in the era is unraveled, it's possible to know what the language at that time was really like. A series of flows from the Victorian writers' English to the 20th century James Joyce's English is one of the destinations of British English. Then, the mainstream of the English language and literature was handed over to Americans, because the role of world leader was also handed over to the United States.

23. American English

Cristopher Columbus (1450s-1506) was born in Italy and later became an explorer, who landed on an island near the coast of South America for the first time as a European in 1492. Originally his exploration was done with the help of the Spanish royal family, Kingdom of Castilla. And his descendants continue as the duke of Spain. After Columbus, many other explorers arrived in the Americas, but everyone thought it was India or China. Then, Amerigo Vespucci (1454-1512), an Italian explorer, landed in South America and he declared that it was a whole New World. The Latin name of *Amerigo* is *Americus*, and the feminine of *Americus* is *America*, which became the name of the Americas. The Virginia Company started a colony (Colony of Virginia) in Jamestown, a place named after King James I in 1607. The Netherlands colonized New Amsterdam (later New York) in 1614.

In search of freedom of religion, a group of Puritans who tried to further reform or to cut ties with the Church of England, sailed across the Atlantic and reached North America. Afraid of King James' oppression, the Pilgrim Fathers boarded a ship named *Mayflower* and came to the east coast of America in 1620. And they pioneered the Plymouth Colony (1620-91). The colony of Massachusetts Bay was founded in 1630, making the capital city Boston, New England. Outraged by British colonial policy, Boston Tea Party occurred in 1773. Then they won the American War of Independence (Revolutionary War), and United States declared Independence in 1776.

The settlers living in New England started to move west into the Great Lakes. The people living around Pennsylvania spread throughout the midwestern area, across the Mississippi, and then finally into California, the West

Coast. Those who were living in Virginia and North Carolina moved along the Gulf Coast and ultimately into Texas. This stream forms the formation of three major dialects of American English; Northern, Midland, and Southern. And the Midland dialect is sometimes called General American. Southern American English has still very unique characteristics. It is pronounced by drawling a vowel, which is called the Southern drawl. Also, the second person plural is expressed as "you all" (y'all). These are well-known features of English spoken in southern America.

During the 17th and 18th centuries many French, German, and Scots-Irish people came to America. The British Government also sent many prisoners to America. In the 19th century, people from Ireland (because of the potato famine in the 1840s), Germany, and Italy arrived, so did many Jews from Central Europe. In the 20th century, people from Asia and Spanish-speaking countries came as immigrants. A wide variety of people came from every country in the world. As a result, many new words have been added to American English. For example, *boss, cookie* (Dutch), *chowder, saloon* (French), *dumb, frankfurter, hamburger, kindergarten* (German), *espresso, lasagna, mafia, minestrone, pasta, pizza, spaghetti* (Italian), and c*afeteria, chili, plaza, taco, tornado* (Spanish or Mexican Spanish).

Native Americans (American Indians) have been living in America. Many of them were abused, killed, and enslaved by whites. The population of American Indians had plummeted. They are now protected by protection policies and social security systems. But some of them are still discriminated against and marginalized. However, there are many place names of American Indian origin, for example, *Massachusetts* and *Mississippi. Moose* is also originally an American Indian word.

Noah Webster

English spoken in America is to form a different shape from British English with the times. Noah Webster (1758-1843) compiled a dictionary entitled *An American Dictionary of the English Language* in 1828. He tried to spell as easily as possible and approached the pronunciation. And many of his suggestions are now accepted as American spellings. One of the differences between American English and British English is the spelling. Like centre (British) - center (American) and theatre (British) - theater (American), *re* becomes *er*. Like colour - color and harbour - harbor, *our* becomes *or*. And *catalogue* (British) becomes *catalog* (American), *programme* (British) becomes *program* (American), and *traveller* (British) becomes *traveler* (American).

Besides, even if it is the same word, many things have different meanings. Thousands of words are used differently. For example, *mad* in American English means *angry* in British English. However, this was originally used in England in the 17th century to mean *angry,* but it is one of the examples that the old-fashioned usage in the UK remained in the USA.

Autumn (British) - fall (American), biscuit (B) - cookie (A, from Dutch), coach (B) - bus (A), chips (B) - French fries (A), crisps (B) - potato chips (A), dustbin (B) - trash can (A), first floor (B) - second floor (A), flat (B) - apartment (A), garage (B) - service station (A), handbag (B) - purse (A), jam(B) - jelly (A), lift (B) - elevator (A), lorry (B) - truck (A), motorway (B) - freeway (A), petrol (B) - gas (gasoline, A), porridge (B) - oatmeal (A), postal code/postcode (B) - zip code (A), public school (B) - private school (A), public toilet (B) - restroom (A), purse (B) - wallet (A), queue (B) - line (A), rubber (B) - eraser (A), underground (B) - subway (A), and so on.

Regarding pronunciation, Americans tend to pronounce *r* with emphasis. Americans pronounce *a* as the short vowel, on the other hand, the British pronounce it as the long vowel, in such words as *bath* [bǽɵ] (America), [bɑ́:ɵ] (Britain), *castle* [kǽsl] (America), [kɑ́:sl] (Britain), *data* [déɪtə] [dǽtə] (America), [dɑ́:tə] (Britain), *last* [lǽst] (America), [lɑ́:st] (Britain), and *participate* [pərtísəpèɪt] (America), [pɑ:rtísəpèɪt] (Britain). Actually, this is one of the dialects of Northern England in the 17th century. Besides, American English tends to be pronounced according to the spelling. Also, Americans tend to pronounce a word as it is spelled. For example, author [ɑ́:ɵər] *daughter* [dɑ́:tər], *launch* [lɑ́:ntʃ], *gawk* [gɑ́:k], *hawk* [hɑ́:k]. On the other hand, Americans pronounce *fillet* or *often* as [filéɪ], [ɔ́fn]. Like this, the *f* sound disappears. Americans say *duke* [dú:k], *news* [nú:z], *Tuesday* [tú:zdeɪ]. The incidence of the semi-vowel *h* sound before *w* in a word like *what* [hwɑ́:t], *when* [hwén], where, whether, which, white, etc. is confirmed in American English. The British pronounce *what* [wɑ́:t][wət] and *when* [wén].

Besides, there is a tendency to use idioms a lot, without using difficult words as a feature of American English. Americans often use "to give up", "to kick the bucket", "to play ball with", "to put off," "to strike out" or "to work over" instead of "to abandon", "to die", "to cooperate with", "to postpone", "to fail", and "to redo".

Nowadays, New York City English is the most popular dialect in America because it's the largest city in the

Harvard University

country, where the United Nations Headquarters is located, and the center of politics, economy, culture, fashion, and entertainment around the world. Major features of the dialect are a high gliding vowel in words like *talk*, *thought*, and *all*. New Yorkers say "stand *on* line", whereas other Americans, "stand *in* line". They tend to speak fast, stand closer, talk louder, and leave shorter pauses between exchanges when they are communicating. They always want to show interest and enthusiasm to their conversation partners.

Now let me check American literary works, the crystal of the language of the country, and a treasure trove of words and knowledge.

Washington Irving (1783-1859) is said to be the first professional writer in the United States to live by the royalties on his books. His representative work is, certainly, *The Sketch Book* (1820) in which one of the most famous short stories, 'Rip Van Winkle' was included. The following are the important works of leading American literature writers. If you read a fragment of these novels, you could feel what kind of English was used at that time. I would like you to taste vivid American English. Typical examples are:

Ralph W. Emerson (1803-82) *Nature* (1836)

Henry D. Thoreau (1817-62) *Walden, or Life in the Woods* (1854)

Edgar Allan Poe (1809-49) *The Fall of the House of Usher* (1839)

Nathaniel Hawthorne (1804-64) *The Scarlet Letter* (1850)

Herman Melville (1819-91) *Moby Dick; or The Whale* (1851)

Walt Whitman (1819-92) *Leaves of Grass* (1855)

Mark Twain (1835-1910) *Adventures of Huckleberry Finn* (1884)

Henry James (1843-1916) *The Turn of the Screw* (1898), *The Ambassadors* (1903)

Sherwood Anderson (1876-1941) *Winesburg, Ohio* (1919)

Francis Scott Fitzgerald (1896-1940) *The Great Gatsby* (1925)

Ernest Miller Hemingway (1899-1961) *The Sun Also Rises* (1926)

William Faulkner (1897-1962) *The Sound and the Fury* (1929)

John Steinbeck (1902-68) *The Grapes of Wrath* (1939)

J. D. Salinger (1919-2010) *The Catcher in the Rye* (1951)

Jack Kerouac (1922-69) *On the Road* (1957)

James Baldwin (1924-87) *The Fire Next Time* (1963)

Here, I would like to introduce the original texts of two leading writers in the United States in particular from the list above. First of all, it's Mark Twain's *Adventures of Huckleberry Finn*. Hemingway also said that all modern American literature began with the work. In this novel, the author denied the traditional European or British novel methods, reproduced the slang and black English used in the United States at the time, and decided the direction of subsequent American literature. First, it's Twain's *Adventures of Huckleberry Finn*, which is indispensable when talking about American literature.

...Her sister, Miss Watson, a tolerable slim old maid, with goggles on, had just come to live with her, and took a set at me now with a spelling-book. She worked me middling hard for about an hour, and then the widow made her ease up. I couldn't stood it much longer. Then for an hour it

Mark Twain

was deadly dull, and I was fidgety. Miss Watson would say, "Don't put your feet up there, Huckleberry;" and "don't scrunch up like that, Huckleberry - set up straight;" and pretty soon she would say, "Don't gap and stretch like that, Huckleberry - why don't you try to behave?" Then she told me all about the bad place, and I said I wished I was there. She got mad then, but I didn't mean no harm. All I wanted was to go somewheres; all I wanted was a change, I warn't particular.[18]

The second is from the representative work of Ernest Miller Hemingway (1899-1961), who participated in World War I, was injured, and fell in love with a nurse at a hospital in Milan, Italy. His hobbies such as drinking and eating with avant-garde artists in Paris, watching bullfighting in Spain, and hunting in Africa, greatly changed the lifestyles of not only American young people but also the people around the world in the 20th century. *The Sun Also Rises* (1926), a brilliant expression of the sense of emptiness after World War I, is a bestseller of the time, and a masterpiece among the works he wrote in the first half of his

Ernest Miller Hemingway

life as a writer. A concise and dry writing style called "hard-boiled" is austerely expressed. That is, the repetition of the same simple word, the use of many proper nouns, the exclusion of the adjectives, adverbs, and abstract words, the suppression of emotional expressions, the attitude of expressing thought by the behavior of a character, attaching importance of the place name, street name, café bar name, and liquor name, and the symbolism of using such words, were major features of the form that had a great influence on later world literature. His literary world conveys a strong message that human consciousness and spirit are not formed by metaphysical ideas such as gods or eternity, but are determined by the materials surrounding him. In fact, Hemingway's thought tended to be materialism from the beginning of his writing career. His novel dealing with Spanish Civil War, *For Whom the Bell Tolls* (1940) was read by many revolutionary soldiers as a textbook on guerrilla warfare, and Hemingway spent the second half of his writing life in Cuba. Considering that Santiago, the protagonist of his masterpiece *The Old Man and the Sea* (1952), is Cuban, Hemingway's attachment to Cuba, disappointment with American dream, and a preference for communism can be seen everywhere. Hemingway won the Nobel Prize in Literature for *The Old Man and the Sea* in 1954. It is said that Hemingway's literature even set the direction of American English after that. Without a doubt, Hemingway is a symbol of American literature and he is not only one of the greatest writers of American literature but also he is one of leading masters of world literature. The following quote is from the ending part of *The Sun Also Rises*, which is a favorite of Hemingway's fans.

…Downstairs we came out through the first-floor dining-room to the street. A waiter went for a taxi. It was hot and bright. Up the street was a little square with trees and grass where there were taxis parked. A taxi came up the street, the waiter hanging out at the side. I tripped him and told the driver where to drive, and got in beside Brett. The driver started up the street. I settled back. Brett moved close to me. We sat close against each other. I put my arm round her and she rested against me comfortably. It was very hot and bright, and the houses looked sharply white. We turned out onto the Gran Via. 'Oh, Jake,' Brett said, 'we could have had such a damned good time together.' Ahead was a mounted policeman in khaki directing traffic. He raised his baton. The car slowed, suddenly pressing Brett against me. 'Yes,' I said. 'Isn't it pretty to think so?' [19]

Today, British English and American English are the two major dialects of the English language. These two continue to influence the world's English. In recent years, American English has swept the world in place of British English by the bottomless strong influence of the United States politically, economically, and militarily. The British Empire first made English an international language in the 19th century. And now USA, the strongest nation all over the world, which reigns at the top of the world, has made English an international language again. And now thousands of American words came into British English.

Most Americans' characters are outgoing, aggressive, and interested in business. They like to debate and think it's embarrassing not to have their own opinion. Such American qualities also give English some kind of characteristics. English will become more and more reasonable and rational. If we unravel the history of America, we can easily understand that people from so many different countries all over the world flowed in and gathered. Then, the United States of America was established. English is the only common language they use to communicate. English spoken in the USA has already been further refined as a mini-international language.

24. Black English

Black English is now called African-American English. But here, we will use the traditional words, Black English. The first African slaves arrived in Virginia in 1619. Then in the 17th century, many black slaves were shipped from West Africa to America. And then, after the American Civil War (1861-65), over 4 million African slaves eventually became free. Sometimes they say, "He come," "She good," "When he say that?"; they don't say, "He's coming," "She's good," "When does he say that?" Or they might say, "I been thinking about that," "An I ain't no plan," instead of "I was thinking about that," "And I haven't no plan." They could say, using "ain't" and "double negatives," "I ain't got no chance," instead of "I don't have any chance," or "I have no chance." *Cool* meaning *excellent* was born from Black English. The slow English of whites living in the South of America may have been one way for them to communicate with blacks. The relationship between whites and blacks gave birth to Southern American English. Considering the history of American literature, the great writer Mark Twain's works showed a lot of Black English. They were valuable linguistic materials which had never been delt with in European literature.

From the end of the 19th century to the beginning of the 20th century, a new music genre called jazz was born, which fused black folk music with European music, mainly in New Orleans, a port city in the southern United States. Simplicity, motif arrangements, ad-libs, improvisations, and "call and response," are characteristics of the music. Jazz soon became popular not only with black musicians but also with white people. Later, many white jazz players' songs were released. As a result, jazz and blues (songs that express

Duke Ellington playing jazz   White jazz band, O.D.J.B.

melancholy, loneliness, and sadness) have a great influence on American culture and also on how to use English words. American English became more and more simplified under the influence of jazz.

No one to talk to

All by myself

No one to walk with

I'm happy on the shelf

Ain't misbehavin'

Savin' all my love for you

"Ain't Misbehavin" (1929) by Andy Razaf

Now you say you're lonely

You cry the long night through

Well, you can cry me a river

Cry me a river

I cried a river over you

"Cry Me A River" (1953) by Arthur Hamilton

It was not long before Black people created a new genre of Black Music which would have a major impact on world music. Then many black music stars appeared in the U.S.A. The African-American musicians introduced here are some of the members of "We Are The World" in 1985. They are Harry Belafonte (1927-), Ray Charles (1930-2004), Tina Turner (1939-), Al Jarreau (1940-2017), Dionne Warwick (1940-), Smokey Robinson (1940-), Diana Ross (1944-), Lionel Richie (1949-), Stevie Wonder (1950-), and Michael Jackson (1958-2009).

"We Are The World" was a campaign song, performed by top African-American artists and others who succeeded in the U.S. White musicians and black musicians got together in order to save those suffering from starvation and poverty in Africa. The main producer was Quincy Jones (1933-), who is a jazz musician and one of black music gurus. The total sales were $63 million, all of which were donated for African children. The lyrics of this song, which convey a straight message, are very simple and accurate in English.

> We are the world, we are the children
>
> We are the ones who make a brighter day
>
> So let's start giving
>
> There's a choice we're making
>
> We're saving our own lives
>
> It's true we'll make a better day
>
> Just you and me
>
> "We Are The World" (1985) by Michael Jackson & Lionel Richie

25. Canadian English

About 15,600 years ago, some race came to Canada from the Eurasian continent. They were Asian and later called Eskimo or Inuit. In fact, they were genetically the same Mongoloid as the Japanese. They captured animals to eat meat and turned their skins into clothes. Some groups of them spread to various parts of present-day Canada, chasing buffalos or chasing whales, eating salmon, or pioneering forests to farm and settle. They were called Aboriginal peoples and now called First Nations. They went further south and when they reached the current USA, they became to be called Native American. And their movement never stopped. They arrived at the current Mexico and then finally they reached South America, where are now Peru, Brazil, Bolivia, Argentina, Chile, etc.

Canada is now the second largest country in the world after Russia, 30 times as large as Japan. In 1867, the British North America Act was passed by the British Parliament, and four colonies such as Nova Scotia, New Brunswick, Lower Canada (now the province of Québec), and Upper Canada (now the province of Ontario), became the Dominion of Canada. In 1982, it became a new

Parliament Hill, Ottawa in 1868

nation completely independent of the United Kingdom. The people who can speak English as a mother-tongue are only 8% of the population. However, across Canada, 60% people use English for their daily life, 20% people use French, and 20% people are bilingual who can speak both English and French. Canada is a multiracial country where British and French culture coexist, and advocates multiculturalism. The population is made up of 77% European whites, 4% indigenous, 3% black, and 16% Asian and other races. The country name Canada comes from an indigenous Iroquois word, *kanata*, which means "village." Perhaps, because the word ends with *a*, it was judged to be a suitable name for a country that evokes the image of femaleness, such as Americ*a*, Argentin*a*, Colombi*a*, and so on. When it comes to religion, we can see that 43% are Catholic, 30% are Protestant, and 1.6% are Orthodox churches and other religious groups.

The capital city is Ottawa, almost on the border of the Anglo-French cultural sphere. More than 60% of citizens of Ottawa speak English, 15% speak French, and many are bilingual. Paul Anka (1941-), a singer-songwriter, who later became very famous in the United States, is from Ottawa. There are many other major cities in Canada. First, the most populous city is Toronto. Its name means "underwater groves" or "a place where people gather," in the words of the indigenous Canadian Aboriginal people (First Nations). In the 19th century, the Irish immigrated to Toronto numerously by the potato famine. Since then, many races landed on Canada and came to Toronto. For example, Germans, Dutch, Italians, Jews, Russians, Poles, Norwegians, Swedes, Portuguese, Chinese, Filipinos, Vietnamese, and Arabs, not to mention English, Scottish and Welsh people. Whites are about half of the population. Most citizens use English language. Next, Canada's second populous city is Montreal. The name of the city comes from the mountain's name, Mont Réal (Royal Mountain), which had been named by a French explorer, Jacques Cartier. Here, 70% of the residents can use French as their first language, and the official language is French only. The majority of the citizens are French-Canadian. Then, Canada's third-largest city is Vancouver, located on the Pacific side. It is a city where as the official language, they use English and French, but actually English is spoken by most inhabitants. The name of the city is derived from British explorer George Vancouver (1757-98). Quebec City, meaning a narrow place in indigenous language, use only French as the official language. In the city, there is a historical district called Old Québec with stone-walls that were used as a military fortress before. There used to be a fierce battle between Britain and France around the town. Of course, it is a world cultural heritage.

Canada spent the colonial eras of both Britain and France in the 17th century, and after the Seven Years War, a French colony called New France, became a British colony. It meant that Canada became part of British North America in 1763. During the American War of Independence (1775-83), a large group of British Loyalists (about 50,000) opposed to American independence and escaped to British territory in Canada. And their English became the basis of what is now Canadian English. In fact, Canadian English is like a mixture of American English and British English, but it has a lot of British English

spellings. But, as for the pronunciation, it's mainly American English. I would like to show some examples of the difference between them: *apartment* (American, Canadian) *flat* (British), *canceled* (A) *cancelled* (B, C), *center* (A) *centre* (B, C), *color* (A) *colour* (B, C), *elevator* (A, C) *lift* (B), *tire* (A, C) *tyre* (B), and so on. Other linguistic features of Canadian English are that they often say "*eh?*" at the end of a sentence, like

Lucy Maud Montgomery   this, "It's fine, eh?" (It's fine, isn't it?)

One of the leading writers of Canadian literature would be Lucy Maud Montgomery (1874-1942), the author of *Anne of Green Gables* (1908), a very famous work. It is said that her ancestors are Scottish and English. Alice Ann Munro (1931-), a short story writer known for *Dance of the Happy Shades* (1968), became the first Canadian writer to win the Nobel Prize in Literature in 2013. Her ancestors are also from Scotland. The following quote is from *Dance of the Happy Shades* by Alice Munro.

> …To Miss Marsalles such a thing is acceptable, but to other people, people who live in the world, it is not. Never mind, they must say something and so they speak gratefully of the music itself, saying how lovely, what a beautiful piece, what is it called? "The Dance of the Happy Shades," says Miss Marsalles. *Danse des ombres heureuses*, she says, which leaves nobody any wiser.[20]

'The Dance of the Happy Shades' is a moving short story that children with disabilities play the piano in a small recital held at the piano teacher's home. However, the story is full of dark, stagnant, and negative-minded adults. The anticlimactic atmosphere is depicted coldly through the eyes of a girl who has reached adolescence. On the other hand, the words used in the story are basically British English spellings, such as *colours* and *programmes*. It is also visible that proper nouns related to the Scottish royal family, for example, Mary Queen of Scots, a tragic Scottish queen and Holyrood Castle, a Scottish royal palace in Edinburgh, are also scattered in the text. After all, it seems to be really Canadian literature to put a French sentence in the last important scene of the story as I introduced it in the quotation above.

26. Australian English

Captain Cook commanded *Endeavour* to Australia and New Zealand

Australia is famous for kangaroos and Aussie beef with a huge continent located in the Southern Hemisphere. Its land is more than 20 times larger than Japan. Kangaroo means "jumping" in the indigenous language *gangurru*. The country was established in 1913, and the capital, Canberra, which means "meeting place" or "place for people" in Aboriginal word *Kambera*, is between Sydney, Australia's most populous city, and Melbourne, the second populous city. Australia used to advocate White Australia and block the acceptance of people from Asia, but now it raises multi-culturalism and aims for its Asianization to integrate with East Asia. The government accepts many Asian immigrants and promotes English education for them.

If we look at the history of Australia, we can see the following: the Dutch first discovered the west side of the continent in 1606, then they named the land

The University of Sydney

New Holland. After that, the Dutch explorers came to investigate several times under the orders of East India Company, but everyone judged the land barren and did not have any interest. In 1770, Captain Cook (1728-79) of the Royal Navy came to the Australian continent and landed in the east, then he named the place New South Wales, declaring that the place was the property of England. At that time, it was not known whether the western part, which the Dutch discovered, was connected to the eastern part where Cook landed or whether it was a separate continent. It was in 1829 that Britain declared its territory throughout Australia. Britain lost America due to the American Revolution War (1775-83) and lost the prisoner destinations it had been doing since 1717. Then, it was Australia that became the place to send criminals instead of America. In 1788, about 750 prisoner men and women were first transported from England to Australia. Sydney was the first penal colony. Since then, about 130,000 people were sent until 1840. However, some criminals, in addition to political prisoners, became exile prisoners just by stealing a piece of handkerchief or a slice of bread. It is said that the majority of the women were prostitutes. Many immigrants, including "free" settlers, used Cockney dialect and Irish English. By 1900, the population of Australia was about 4 million. Australians often use their slang, for example, *Aussie* for *Australian*. Cockney is also widely used, but radio and television announcers and newscasters don't speak Cockney. Australians speak British English basically, but after World War II, they are influenced by American English very much.

Aborigine is now called Aboriginal Australians. The theory that they came from India and settled in 50,000 to 60,000 years ago is predominant. When European people came to Australia, about 500,000 indigenous people were living the same way as the Stone Age. They were hunting with boomerangs. They were robbed of the sacred land by

Sydney Opera House

Julia Gillard, Australia's first
female Prime Minister

whites. They were poisoned, slaughtered as Sport Hunting, and starved to death. According to a 1920 survey, their population had dropped to 60,000. Later, in 1951, they were allowed to live in the same conditions as white people, and citizenship was granted in 1967.

Evonne Goolagong (1951-) is an Aboriginal female tennis player who won the Wimbledon Women's Singles twice (1971, 1980) and the Women's Doubles in 1974. Catherine Freeman (1973-), who won gold in the women's 400 meters at the Sydney Olympics (2000), is also of Aboriginal origin.

It is said that the native language of Aborigines didn't have much effect on Australian English except for the names of animals such as *kangaroo, koala, wallaby*. Instead of "Hello!" sometimes they say, "Good day," or "G'day." Also, like British English, they use "Sorry" instead of "Pardon?" or "Excuse me."

Australia's first female Prime Minister is Julia Gillard (1961-), who was born in Wales, U.K., and moved to Australia at the age of five. She served the nation as Prime Minister from 2010 to 2013.

'I'd been away from home for eight years,' said Mitchell to his mate, as they dropped their swags in the mulga shade and sat down. 'I hadn't written a letter — kept putting it off, and a blundering fool of a fellow that got down the day before me told the old folks that he'd heard I was dead.' Here he took a pull at his water-bag.[21]

This is the opening part of the sketch story, 'On the Edge of a Plain' (1893) written by Australian writer Henry Lawson (1867-1922), beginning with "I'd been away from home for eight years," and this is an echo of common feelings about their homeland for people who came to Australia from England. A tree named *mulga*, also suggests that the setting of this story should be in Australia. The name of the main character is Mitchell, which is reminiscent of the angel Michael, but ironically Mitchell is a criminal. There is a casual conversation in the grove,

Henry Lawson

but something wrong was done by the two men. The story conveys the image of the fact that Australia used to be the place for prisoners from Britain. Outlaws like those who appeared in the western part of the USA may have threatened the security of the country. The term *a blundering fool of a fellow* is also impressive because it seems to be rough and ill-mannered. The word *water-bag* indicates how important water is in Australia. In this short story, the word water appears five times. Most of the land is desert, and not getting drinking water is life-threatening. However, at the end of the story, two rogues show a personality that cannot be hated, somehow. They watered an injured puppy, showing an extremely kind-hearted attitude. I think this short story is a very likable work that expresses the lovable character of Australians.

27. New Zealand English

In the 9th century, the Polynesian people began to migrate to the land and became indigenous peoples known as Māori. They are now 12% of the population. The country was originally called Nieuw Zeeland in Dutch named after Province Zeeland in southwestern Netherlands. It is Nova Zeelandia (zee means sea) in Latin. Later, it was spelled in English. At the request of the Dutch East India Company, in 1642 a Dutch explorer, Abel Tasman (1603-59) came to the area of Australia to investigate. Initially, he discovered Tasmania, an island in the southwestern part of Australia, but missed the main Australian continent. He went east, becoming the first European to arrive on New Zealand's South Island. Later, in October 1769, Captain Cook (1728-79) landed in New Zealand as the second European. Cook conducted a detailed survey of the island. In the 1790s, whalers and traders started to settle in New Zealand. In 1840, a treaty was signed and the first British colony was established. In 1907, it became the Dominion of New Zeeland and became completely independent of the United Kingdom. Many emigrated from New South Wales, the southeastern part of Australia. Since 1841,

Auckland, the country's largest city

the capital had been Auckland, but in 1865, moved to Wellington, the second biggest city, because Auckland was too close to the north. Wellington was named after the Duke of Wellington, the British commander who won over Napoleon's army in the Battle of Waterloo in 1815. Christchurch, the third-largest city, was named after Christ Church College, Oxford University.

In the 1960s, New Zealand became one of the wealthiest countries in the world. The New Zealanders insisted that only America, Canada, and Sweden were better. Their country is now a working man's paradise, exporting wool, meat (lamb and beef), butter, cheese, timber, and kiwifruit to the world. In addition, more than 2.6 million tourists visit New Zealand each year from all over the world.

The New Zealand Rugby Football Union was established in 1892. Since then, the national team, nicknamed "All Blacks," has won three World Cups. Before the game, *Haka*, the traditional Māori dance is always performed by the players. One of the national symbols of New Zealand is a flightless bird, *kiwi*, which often refers to New Zealanders, but it doesn't mean contempt.

Looking at women's social advancement, it seems that women's activities in New Zealand stand out. Ethel Benjamin (1875-1943) was the first female lawyer, and she was admitted to the Bar in Dunedin. Her parents had emigrated from England. There are many female painters from New Zealand, for example, Dolla Richmond (1861-1935), Frances Hodgkins (1869-1947), and Mollie Tripe (1870-1939). And now, there are many female teachers, doctors, lawyers, accountants, and architects. Since 2017, the Prime Minister of New Zealand is Jacinda Ardern (1980-). She became Prime Minister at the age of 37. Before her, there were two female Prime Ministers: Jennifer Shipley (1952-) and Helen Clark (1950-).

New Zealand English is also known as Kiwi English, but it's basically British English. They pronounce *can't* [ká:nt] and *castle* [ká:sl]. They spell *defence*, *harbour*, and *theatre*. Americans say *downtown*, *gas*, and *take out*, but New Zealanders say *city centre*, *petrol*, and *take away*. They often say "*eh?*" at the end of a sentence, just like Canadian English. Influenced by Māori, they say, "Kia Ora." instead of "Hello." The names of the flora and fauna are from Māori language. Auckland, the largest city, is made up of multi-ethnic people, so the English spoken in the area is also very different. There were many Scottish settlers in the south part of the South Island, where it is said that Scottish vocabulary and pronunciation still remain.

> ...Laura was terribly nervous. Tossing the velvet ribbon over her shoulder, she said to a woman standing by, 'Is this Mrs Scott's house?' and the woman, smiling queerly, said, 'It is, my lass.'
>
> ....
>
> 'I say, you're not crying, are you?' asked her brother. Laura shook her head. She was. Laurie put his arm round her shoulder. 'Don't cry,' he said in his warm, loving voice. 'Was it awful?' 'No,' sobbed Laura. 'It was simply marvellous. But, Laurie—' She stopped, she looked at her brother. 'Isn't life,' she stammered, 'isn't life—' But what life was she couldn't explain. No matter. He quite understood. 'Isn't it, darling?' said Laurie.[22]

This is part of a short story titled 'The Garden Party' (1921) by Katherine Mansfield (1888-1923). She is the most well-known New Zealand writer. She wrote this story two years before she died. She had been plagued by ill health and passed away at the age of 34. There is no doubt that 'The Garden Party' is a masterpiece in her work based on New Zealand. In the middle of the story, the *karaka*, New Zealand laurel, appears symbolically, and it suggests that the story is set in New Zealand. Its name is Māori language, and its orange-colored fruit is also Māori food. It's also the Māori term for the color orange. Regarding Mansfield's writing style, for example, using words spelled like *Mrs* and *marvellous*, or using single quotation marks, it shows the characteristics of British English. It also suggests that the use of the words like *Scott* and *lass* is reminiscent of people from Scotland. While reading this piece, we can easily remember the image of Jane Austen's literary world. It depicts the lovely daily life of the middle-class

Katherine Mansfield

people living in New Zealand from the perspective of a young girl. However, unlike Austen (1775-1817), Mansfield is dealing with life and death in her story. Just before the party starts, there is a dispute about whether to cancel the party, inserting an episode of the crash death of a poor man (possibly from Scotland) on the day of the party. In the end, it is done as scheduled, and they will try to solve the problem by delivering what is left uneaten to the house of the dead. And finally, ask the reader what death is and what life is, and the story ends.

It is clear that Mansfield's writing style was influenced by the stream of consciousness that James Joyce (1882-1941) and Virginia Woolf (1882-1941) had succeeded. Ian A. Gordon (1908-2004) pointed out her skill of "interior monologue" in *Katherine Mansfield: Writers and their work* (1967). We can admit that 'The Garden Party' is a highly complete work, repeatedly depicting sympathy for workers of different classes. It suggests even the relationship between Europeans and Māori people in New Zealand.

28. English spoken in India

The name of India comes from the ancient Greek word for Indus River, around which the Indus Valley Civilization flourished between 2600 BC and 1800 BC. India is famous for being the birthplace of Buddhism, but Hinduism is the largest, with one billion Hindus. Now, the capital city is Delhi and the largest city is Mumbai, which was called Bombay (Good-bay) before. India has a strong impact on the world in various areas now, for example, a military power, a nuclear power, regional power, and the economic power after the United States and China.

In 1600, the British East India Company was established. In 1858, Britain dissolved the Company and made India a colony under the direct control of the United Kingdom. In 1877, Queen Victoria became Empress of India. In 1947, under the political guidance of Mahātmā Gandhi (1869-1948) and other people, India became independent from the United Kingdom. Gandhi's non-violent resistance, civil disobedience, and economic or political noncooperation were extremely effective.

Agra Fort built in 1573 by Akbar I, India's greatest king

Nearly 1.4 billion people are said to be the second-largest population in the world after China but will be the first by 2025, overtaking China. Hindi is the official language, and English is the quasi-official language based on British English. According to a 2007 survey by Miniwatts Marking Group,

12% of the population speaks English, and the number of English-speaking people is second only to that of the United States. Indians tend to pronounce English words as they are spelled, for example, *Wednesday* [wédnezdei]. The word *tha* is pronounced as [tǽ] or [dǽ], for example, *thank* [tǽŋk] or *that* [dǽt]. They tend to pronounce the *r*

Khushwant Singh

sound emphatically, for example, *after* [ǽftəru], *park* [pá:ruk]. Vowel sounds are pronounced after the consonant sound, for example, *but* [bəto], *hot* [há:to]. They say, "What is your good name?" instead of "What is your name?". There are many expressions in English spoken by Indians as follows: "I am knowing it", "I'm having a hat", "I'm understanding it", "You are American, no?", "He is Paul, correct?", etc.

Khushwant Singh (1915-2014) was a popular historical novelist, and wrote many books in English. His masterpiece is *Delhi: A Novel* (1990). Here are the beginning and the ending parts of the extraordinary long historical novel.

I return to Delhi as I return to my mistress Bhagmati when I have had my fill of whoring in foreign lands. Delhi and Bhagmati have a lot in common. Having been long misused by rough people they have learnt to conceal their seductive charms under a mask of repulsive ugliness. It is only to their lovers, among whom I count myself, that they reveal their true selves.[23]

....

A boy gets a car tyre, fills its inside rim with petrol and lights it. It is a fiery garland. Two boys hold it over Budh Singh and slowly bring it down over his head to his shoulders. Budh Singh screams in agony as he crumples down to the ground. The boys laugh and give him the Sikh call of victory: *'Boley So Nihal! Sat Sri Akal.'* [24]

First, the author starts the story likening Delhi, the capital of India, to a mistress, and finally, the story ends with the atrocities (killing every Sikh in the city) of Hindu boys due to Indira Gandhi's assassination at the hands of her own Sikh bodyguards. The heroine's name *Bhagmati* is reminiscent of the Bagmati River which joins the Ganges (Ganges River). *Singh* is a typical name given to Sikh boys. The English used here is basically British English as the writer uses *learnt*, *tyre*, and *petrol* instead of *tire*, *learned*, and *gas*. The word *fill* appears at the beginning of the story, and the word *fills* appears at the end of the story. These two words affect each other. This work is a requiem for a historic city that has lost many traditions and memories so much.

Taj Mahal built in 1653 by Emperor Shah Jahan in memory of his wife's death

Gandhi (right) talking with Nehru (left)

29. English spoken in Singapore

Singapore is a multiracial nation made up of Chinese (80%), Malay, Indian, and other races. Chinese, Malay, Tamil, and English are the official languages. The country name is Sanskrit, meaning Lion City. It was established in 1819 with the permission of Johor Sultanate as a trading place for the British East India Company. In 1824, it became a British colony. In 1832, it became the capital of Straits Settlements. During World War II (1942-45), Singapore was occupied by the Empire of Japan. In 1963, Malaysia became independent from the United Kingdom, and Singapore became part of the federation of Malaysia. In 1965, it became independent as the Republic of Singapore. It was a British colony for about 150 years, and English has been used for a long time.

English became the official language to connect Chinese, Malays, Indians, and others in the business world. Today, Singapore is the center of trade, transportation, finance, education, entertainment, tourism, and innovation, not only in Asia but also around the world. They use English as the common language. At the same time, in parallel with official English, Singapore Standard English was born among the common people. The language is very unique and it is called Singlish. The characteristic of Singlish is a mixture of English, Chinese and Malay. Verbs are sometimes used in succession due to Malay influences. It also simplifies tense, omits articles, be-verbs, and third-person singular "s," and all nouns

Singapore tourism icon, Merlion

Marina Bay Sands

are singular and have no *s* in the plural form. For example, "There are three *cat*." They use "lah" a lot at the end of the sentence to emphasize the meaning. For example, "Difficult lah." means "It's very difficult, isn't it?" They say, "What happen yesterday?" instead of "What happened yesterday?", "I go tomorrow." instead of "I will go tomorrow.", "You go where?" instead of "Where do you go?", "He eat what?" instead of "What does he eat?", "He so cool." instead of "He's so cool.", "Why you so loose in time?" instead of "Why are you so loose in time?", and "Discount can?" instead of "Can I discount?". When you are asked, "Can you...?", your answer may be "Can." for "Yes, I can." and "Can't." for "No, I can't." When you pronounce "th", it is pronounced with the sound of [t] or [d]. For example, "thing" is [tíŋ], and "they" is [déɪ]. The Singaporean Government has taken various policies to expel this Singlish, but the public is still familiar with Singlish. Some scholars point out that Singlish has a future look at English.

"Wait a minute—I'm in first class. Take me to first class," Edison Cheng said contemptuously to the flight attendant escorting him to his seat. "This is first class, Mr. Cheng," the man in the crisp navy uniform informed him. "But where are the cabins?" Eddie asked, still confused. "Mr. Cheng, I'm afraid British Airways does not have private cabins in first class. But if you'd allow me to show you some of the special features of your seat—" "No, no, that's fine." Eddie tossed his ostrich leather briefcase onto the seat like a petulant schoolboy.[25]

This is a quote from *China Rich Girlfriend* (2015) written by Kevin Kwan, the current popular writer living in the United States. He was born in Singapore and moved to the USA when he was a teenager. He is a young trendy writer now. One of his works *China Rich Girlfriend* is a sequel to *Crazy Rich Asians* (2013), which became a bestseller and was made into a movie in the United States in 2018. Kwan also published *Rich People Problems* (2017), and three works became Kwan's trilogy.

Arab Street, one of the most popular tourist spots in multi-ethnic Singapore

30. English spoken in South Africa

Slavery was abolished in 1833, but discrimination continued in South Africa. However, in 1994, Nelson Mandela (1918-2013) became the first black president, officially eliminating Apartheid of black racism (including mixed-race people and Indians).

In 1795, the British occupied the Dutch colony of Cape Town. In 1822, English became the official language. But the number of Dutch-speaking people was very large. Then, more and more British arrived there in search of diamonds and gold, especially in the 1870s. The ratio of whites to blacks in South Africa is now one to eight. And the black majority speak Dutch (Afrikaans), which was given official status in 1925. South African-born whites also use Afrikaans. So English is still a minority language. Even now, South African English is strongly influenced by British English. The percentage of native English speakers is 10%. Currently, 30% of South Africa's population speaks English. They are bilingual in Afrikaans and English.

> I have never seen anything like it: two discs of glass suspended in front of his eyes in loops of wire. Is he blind? I could understand it if he wanted to hide blind eyes. But he is not blind. The discs are dark, they look opaque from the outside, but he can see through them. He tells me they are a new invention. 'They protect one's eyes against the glare of the sun,' he says. [26]

....

I think: 'I wanted to live outside history. I wanted to live outside the history that Empire imposes on its subjects, even its lost subjects. I never wished it for the barbarians that they should have the history of Empire laid upon them. How can I believe that that is cause for shame?'[27]

The quotes above are the opening and final parts of J. W. Coetzee's masterpiece *Waiting for the Barbarians* published in 1980. Of course, this title is an echo of Samuel Beckett's *En attendant Godot* ("Waiting for Godot") published in 1952. Coetzee was born in Cape Town, Union of South Africa, in 1940. He is an Afrikaner who won the Nobel Prize in Literature in 2003. Reading the text, we can notice the word "blind" repeated three times in the first four lines of the novel, and it is clear that the author wanted to say the message that the history of the human race might have been a history of blindness. The story is as follows: A fictional empire (the image of the British Empire) controls a colony built in the desert (we can imagine South Africa), but one day they come to believe the barbarians will attack the fortified town. Military officials imprison innocent local people one after another, treat them below humans, and torture them. And finally, the story ends, hinting that the barbarians are invading the walled town where officers and soldiers had already run away. Changing the viewpoint, we can say that the fear of the barbarians kicked the ruler out of the town. They say the barbarians are coming, but none knows if they are really barbarians. Who the hell are the barbarians? History is a repetition of the struggle between the conquering side and the conquered side, and there is no justice where armed people attack a land. Will the end of human history melt and disappear like a *snowman*? (Coetzee let the main character say, 'It is not a bad snowman,' at the end of the story.) The novel is also made into a film in 2019 by Colombian director Ciro Guerra (1981-). In the movie, grotesque and cruel scenes are repeated on the screen, and some people may not be able to tolerate staring. But it's the creator's intention and we have to understand the dark message of the story.

Zozibini Tsunzi

Nowadays, Coetzee argues that literary people in the Southern Hemisphere (Southern Africa, Australia, New Zealand, and South America) should unite and counter English-centered world literature. He dared to publish the English original version in other foreign languages, such as Spanish, French, and Japanese. In 2006, he became an Australian citizen.

In 2019, Zozibini Tsunzi of South Africa won the Miss Universe 2019 in Atlanta, USA. Zozi said in her final speech, "I grew up in a world where a woman who looks like me, with my kind of skin and my kind of hair, was never considered to be beautiful. I think it is time that that stops today. I want children to look at me and see my face and I want them to see their faces reflected in mine." She was asked what we should be teaching young girls today. She said of leadership: "It's something that has been lacking in young girls and women for a very long time, not because we don't want to, but because of what society has labelled women to be. I think we are the most powerful beings on the world, and that we should be given every opportunity, and that is what we should be teaching these young girls to take up space. Nothing is more important than taking up space in society."

CONCLUSION

English has been the official language for aviation and shipping for a long time. The English language of air communication is called Air-speak and the sea communication English is called Ship-speak. In the academic and research world, English is now the common language, and it has become common to write English papers in all research fields. Of course, English is needed in the fields of global business, economy, and politics. According to David Crystal's *English as a Global Language* (2003) and United Nations statistics (2020), 80% of the films screened around the world are in English. The world's population of English users are 370 million (English as a native language), 350 million (English as a second language), and 750 million (English as a foreign language). So, about 1.5 billion people in total can understand English. About 90% of the population of Netherlands, Norway, and Denmark can speak English. 80% of the population of Singapore, the Philippines, and Israel can speak English. 70% of Austria, 60% of Germany, Switzerland and Belgium, 50% of Pakistan, Greece, and Nigeria, 40% of France and Egypt, and 30% of Italy and Poland can speak English. It is said that only 10% of Japanese can speak English, even though Japan is a trading country and Gross National Product is the third largest in the world after the United States and China. Now, about half of the world's population (7.7 billion) somehow benefits from an English-based system; knowledge and information of the world are accumulated in English.

Internet technology developed in the United States in the 1960s. And since the 1990s, it has spread and had a great influence on commerce, business, and culture all over the world. Of course, the language used on the Internet is basically English, which occupies an immovable position as the Internet language in the world. The number of people who use English on the Internet is about 1.1 billion (25% of users). Meanwhile, Internet users who use Chinese grew to 850 million (19% of users) in 2020. Still, the Internet will be used by an increasing number of English-speaking people worldwide in the future. It is not expected that the number of people who use Chinese on the Internet will increase, because we don't think there will be more people who dare to use the Chinese language on the Internet except Chinese people. The situation of English monopoly in every area of academia, education, art, science and technology, politics, economy, business, sports, and culture will continue for a while. Also, the rapid progress of AI may have some effect on English and we should not overlook the ever-evolving automated translator's diffusion.

In the past, it was the opinion of many linguists that English, which had spread around the world, would eventually evolve its own and grow into a different language rooted in the region. It was as if Latin had become French, Italian, or Spanish, or from Proto-Germanic to German, Dutch, English, Norwegian, Sweden, Danish and Icelandic, just as Singlish was born in Singapore. However, it was a

The old man and his cows

hypothesis before the spread of satellite broadcasting and the Internet that made it possible to connect the world in real time by clear pictures, voice and video. It was utterly an imaginary and needless problem before the situation that the media can continue to send enormous messages to the world at the same time.

We can reinforce it by using the Internet that makes it possible to share news, information and knowledge all over the world. The rise of Britain in the 19th century, the success of America in the 20th century, and the spread of the Internet in the 21st century have increasingly spurred the internationalization of English.

Girls heading for Gandhi's grave

Also, the tendency is uniformity of pronunciation, vocabulary, grammar, and spelling of English, which, spreading around the world, once tended to develop independently in each region. English will not be the same fate as Latin. It will certainly evolve more and more as a global language because English is the language that has been trained by many races for a melting pot. It has been changed and brushed up for a long time in the history, and it became what it should be today. No other languages could be a world language instead of English.

Languages in many countries, including Japanese, are increasingly being used as English words, which symbolically express the culture of every country in the world. Sometimes the word becomes an international language. Here are some typical Japanese words that have already been widely recognized and registered in the dictionary as English: bento, bonsai, dojo, emoji, futon, hara-kiri, haiku, ikebana, kabuki, kamikaze, karaoke, karate, kawaii, kendo, kimono, manga, miso, ninja, nori, origami, otaku, ramen, sake, samurai, senpai, seppuku, shogun, shogunate, sukiyaki, sumo, sushi, tatami, tempura, teriyaki, tofu, tsunami (tidal wave), ukiyo-e, waka, wasabi, and zen.

Compared to Chinese, the most spoken language in the world, and Spanish, the language spoken after English, I think that English has indispensable and sufficient conditions for the world language in every respect. The key words for a language to become international are simplicity, tolerance, conciseness, inclusion, rationality, and sound attraction in terms of pronunciation. English can express complicated contents in simple way with a beautiful tone. And those features are not the ones of others, but the ones of the English language that has progressed and reached those areas in the history of more than 2000 years. English will continue to maintain and refine its proper direction to the all-round language. A language is developing continually and independently, influenced by other languages, so is a human being.

Summer in London

NOTES

(1) George Jack, *Beowulf: A Student Edition* (Oxford University Press, 1994), p.34.

(2) Sir Walter Scott, *Ivanhoe* (Oxford University Press, 1996), p.27.

(3) Hiromichi Nishino, *Igirisu no Kojo wo Tabisuru: Visiting Castles of Britain* (Futaba-sha, 1995), p.30.

(4) Melvyn Bragg, *The Adventure of English: The Biography of a Language* (Hodder & Stoughton, 2003), p.67.

(5) Larry D. Benson, *The Riverside Chaucer* (Third Edition, Oxford University Press, 1988), p.23.

(6) Sir Donald Wolfit and Dr Břetislav Hodek, *The Complete Works of William Shakespeare* (Spring Books, 1981), p.901.

(7) *Ibid.*, p.960.

(8) Charles James Stuart, *The Holy Bible: Authorized King James Version* (Oxford University Press, 1993), p.9.

(9) William Wordsworth and Samuel Taylor Coleridge, *Lyrical Ballads* (Penguin Classics, 1999), pp.111-112.

(10) Jane Austen, *Pride and Prejudice* (Penguin Classics, 1972), p.51.

(11) Charles Dickens, *The Mystery of Edwin Drood* (Penguin Classics, 1985), p.37.

(12) Charlotte Brontë, *Jane Eyre* (Penguin Classics, 1996), p.39.

(13) Arthur Conan Doyle, *Sherlock Holmes Selected Stories* (Oxford University Press, 1951), p.34.

(14) D. H. Lawrence, *Lady Chatterley's Lover* (Wordsworth Classics, 2007), p.1.

(15) Sir Walter Scott, *Waverley* (Penguin Popular Classics, 1994), p.400.

(16) George Bernard Shaw, *Jhon Bull's Other Island* (BiblioBazaar, 2007). p.14.

(17) James Joyce, *Ulysses* (Wordsworth Classics, 2010), p.682.

(18) Mark Twain, *Adventures of Huckleberry Finn* (SeaWolf Press, 2018), p.3.

(19) Ernest Miller Hemingway, *Fiesta: The Sun Also Rises* (Grafton Books, 1987), p.206.

(20) Alice Munro, *Dance of the Happy Shades* (Penguin Random House UK, 2021), pp.231-232.

(21) Henry Lawson, *While The Billy Boils* (Angus and Robertson, 1990), p.32.

(22) Katherine Mansfield, *Selected Stories* (Oxford University Press, 2008), pp.348-349.

(23) Khushwant Singh, *Delhi: A Novel* (Penguin Random House India, 2017), p.1.

(24) *Ibid.*, p.391.

(25) Kevin Kwan, *China Rich Girlfriend* (Anchor Books, 2015), p.3.

(26) J. M. Coetzee, *Waiting for the Barbarians* (Vintage, 2004), p.1.

(27) *Ibid.*, p.169.

BIBLIOGRAPHY

Anderson, James, and G. Ross Roy. *Sir Walter Scott and History*, The Edina Press Lid., 1981.

Bambas, Rudolph C. *The English Language: Its Origin and History*, University of Oklahoma Press, 1980.

Barclay, Isabel. *The Story of Canada*, Pagurian Press Limited, 1974.

Bassett, Judith, Keith Sinclair, and Marcia Stenson. *The Story of New Zealand*, Reed Methuen Publishers Ltd., 1985.

Blake, N. F. *The Language of Shakespeare*, MacMillan Press Ltd., 1989.

Bloom, Harold and Lionel Trilling, *Romantic Poetry and Prose*, Oxford University Press, 1973.

Bowen, Zack. *Critical Essays on Sir Walter Scott: The Waverley Novels*, G. K. Hall & Co., 1996.

Bragg, Melvyn. *The Adventure of English: The Biography of a Language*, Hodder & Stoughton, 2003.

Brantlinger, Patrick, and William B. Thesing. *A Companion to The Victorian Novel*, Blackwell Publishing Lid, 2007.

Brook, G. L. *A History of the English Language*, The Language Library, 1958.

Brook, G. L. *The Language of Shakespeare*, Andre Deutsch, 1976.

Cannon, Garland. *A History of the English Language*, Harcourt Brace Jovanovich, 1972.

Carter, Ronald and John McRae. *Guide to English Literature: Britain and Ireland*, The Penguin, 1996.

Coghill, Nevill. *Geoffery Chaucer The Canterbury Tales*, Penguin Books, 1977.

Craig, Edward. *Philosophy: A Very Short Introduction*, Oxford University Press, 2020.

Crystal, David. *The Cambridge Encyclopedia of the English Language*, Cambridge University Press, 1995.

Crystal, David. *The English Language*, Second Edition, Penguin Books, 2002.

Crystal, David. *English as a Global Language*, Second Edition, Cambridge University Press, 2003.

Deighton, H. S. *The Oxford Introduction to British History: A Portrait of Britain*, Oxford University Press, 1987.

Eagle, Dorothy and Hilary Carnell. *The Oxford Literary Guide to the British Isles*, Oxford University Press, 1977.

English Heritage. *The Blue Plaque Guide*, Journeyman Press, 1991.

Fulk, R. D., Robert E. Bjork, and John D. Niles. *Klaeber's Beowulf*, University of Tronto Press, 2008.

Jeffares, A. Norman. *Scott's Mind and Art*, Oliver & Boyd, 1969.

Johnson, Edgar. *Sir Walter Scott, The Great Unknown, Vol.1, Vol.2*, Hamish Hamilton, 1970.

Johnson, Keith. *Shakespeare's English*, Routledge, 2014.

Kaye, Sharon. *Philosophy: A complete introduction*, Hodder & Stoughton, 2013.

Kaye, Sharon. *The Philosophy Book for Beginners: A Brief Introduction to Great Thinkers and Big Ideas*, Rockridge Press, 2021.

Kenny, Anthony. *A New History of Western Philosophy*, Oxford University Press, 2010.

Kermode, Frank. *Shakespeare's Language*, Penguin Books, 2000.

Kerrigan, John. *The Sonnets and A Lover's Complaint by William Shakespeare*, Penguin Books, 1995.

Lamb, Charles. *Elia, 1823*, Woodstock Books, 1991.

Lindsay, Donald and E. S. Washington. *A Portrait of Britain 1688-1851*, Oxford University Press, 1984.

Lockhart, John Gibson. *The Life of Sir Walter Scott*, Hutchinson & Co., 1848.

McCrum, Robert, William Cran, and Robert MacNeil. *The Story of English: Third Revised Edition*, Faber & Faber, 2002.

Morgan, Kenneth. *Australia: A Very Short Introduction*, Oxford University Press, 2012.

Morpurgo, J. E. *Keats*, Penguin Books, 1985.

Myers, L. M. and Richard L. Hoffman. *The Roots of Modern English*, Second Edition, University of Oklahoma Press, 1980.

Norgate, G. LE Grys. *The Life of Sir Walter Scott*, Methuen & CO., 1906.

Ousby, Ian. *Literary Britain and Ireland*, A & C Black, 1990.

Pearson, Hesketh. *Walter Scott: His Life and Personality*, Methuen & CO. Ltd., 1954.

Price, Mary R. *A Portrait of Britain 1066-1485*, Oxford University Press, 1987.

Price, Mary R. and C. E. L. Mather. *A Portrait of Britain 1485-1688*, Oxford University Press, 1988.

Reed, James. *Sir Walter Scott: Landscape and Locality*, The Athlone Press, 1980.

Russell, Bertrand. *History of Western Philosophy*, Routledge Classics, 1996.

Shaw, Harry E. *Critical Essays on Sir Walter Scott: The Waverley Novels*, G. K. Hall & Co., 1996.

Sutherland, John. *The Life of Walter Scott*, Blackwell Publishers, 1995.

Till, Antonia. *The Collected Poems of William Wordsworth*, Wordsworth Poetry Library, 2006.

Thornley, G.C. and Gwyneth Roberts. *An Outline of English Literature*, Longman, 1993.

Vendler, Helen. *The Art of Shakespeare's Sonnets*, The Belknap Press of Harvard University Press, 1997.

Vicary, Tim. *The Brontë Story*, Oxford University Press, 1991.

Viney, Bright. *The History of the English Language*, Oxford University Press, 2008.

Wilson, A. N. *A Life of Walter Scott*, Mandarin, 1996.

Warburton, Nigel. *A Little History of Philosophy*, Yale University Press, 2011.

AFTERWARD

Originally, most of the content of this book was revised from the paper 'The Future of English Spreading Around the World — From the Perspective of English History — ' submitted to Ryutsu Keizai Daigaku Ronshu (The Journal of Ryutsu Keizai University), Vol. 57, No.1 September, 2022. Regarding Old English and Middle English, two papers, 'The Origin of the English Language' and 'The Encounter between Norman French and Anglo-Saxon' submitted to Tokyo Future University Bulletin 2021 Vol.15 and Bulletin 2022 Vol. 16 were revised and added to this book. David Hume's article is from the paper 'A Study of the Future Vision of Philosophy – From the Perspective of the History of Western Philosophy-' submitted to Ryutsu Keizai Daigaku Ronshu (The Journal of Ryutsu Keizai University), Vol. 57, No.3. January, 2023, with corrections added. Wordsworth's and Walter Scott's parts have been newly written and added. Wordsworth is a poet that my academic supervisor, Professor Yasuo Deguchi (1929-2019) of Waseda University, loved very much. I fondly remember his unique comment and deep interpretation in his graduate school seminar. As for Scott, I have just summarized part of my master's thesis, "A Study of Scott's Sense of History" (January 2000), corrected and added this time.

Most of the photos used in this book were taken by me, the author of this book (p.4, p.8, p.10, p.12, p.14, p.21, p.30, p.31, p.34, p.39, p.42, p.50, p.54, p.57, p.71, p.74, p.77, p.79, p.85, p.86, p.92, p.95, p.140, Ryugasaki Campus of Ryutsu Keizai University, University of Oxford, Summer in London, Afternoon

Tea, University of California, Abbotsford, and Charles Dickens Museum on the cover, and also photos of four Japanese universities where I work for now on the back cover). In addition, some of photos were provided by Professor Hidemi Kobayashi of Ibaraki University (p.65 and Dove Cottage on the cover), Professor Shinya Kawahara of Seinan Gakuin University (p.99, p.103, p.131, p.132, p.133, night view of Singapore with Marina Bay Sands, and the Old Library at Trinity College, Dublin on the cover), Mr. Hideyuki Matsui of Ryutsu Keizai University (p.120 below, p.121, and the University of Sydney on the cover), Mr. Takumi Matsuoka (p.128, p.130 left, p.138, p.139, and Indian girls on the cover), and Mr. Yasumasa Nishino (p.145, Bronze statue of Shakespeare, and William Morris designed curtain on the cover). Others are from the public domain. I would like to take this opportunity to thank everyone for their cooperation. Finally, again, I would like to thank Mr. Ei Onozaki of Ryutsu Keizai University Press.

Hiromichi Nishino

England's rose

ABOUT THE AUTHOR

西野 博道（にしの・ひろみち）

東京都出身。早稲田大学卒業、同大学院修士課程修了。専攻は英語英文学。流通経済大学付属柏高等学校教諭を10年間務めた後、早稲田大学、明治大学、埼玉大学、千葉工業大学、日本体育大学にて英語講読、英会話、ビジネス英語、TOEIC、英語プレゼンテーション等の指導に当たる。早稲田大学では公開講座を年4回7年間にわたり担当。現在、茨城大学、文教大学、東京未来大学、流通経済大学ほか非常勤講師。著書に『イギリスの古城を旅する』（双葉社）『戦略戦術兵器事典⑤ヨーロッパ城郭編』（共著・学習研究社）『美神を追いて－イギリス・ロマン派の系譜』（共著・音羽書房鶴見書店）『21世紀イギリス文化を知る事典』（共著・東京書籍）『スコットランド文化事典』（共著・原書房）のほか『埼玉の城址30選』（埼玉新聞社）『江戸城の縄張りをめぐる』（幹書房）『関東の城址を歩く』『英傑を生んだ日本の城址を歩く』（さきたま出版会）『日本の城郭－築城者の野望』『日本の城郭－名将のプライド』（柏書房）など日英城郭研究の成果を踏まえた著書が多数ある。'The History of Japanese Castles with the Perspective of British Castles'（流通経濟大學論集 2021.10）等はネット公開されているので是非ご覧ください。

The Future of English Spreading Around the World
A Brief History of English Language and Literature

発行日 2023年4月1日 初版発行

著 者 西 野 博 道
発行者 上 野 裕 一
発行所 流通経済大学出版会
〒301-8555 茨城県龍ヶ崎市120
電話 0297-60-1167 FAX 0297-60-1165

©Hiromichi Nishino, 2023

Printed in Japan/アベル社
ISBN978-4-947553-93-5 C0098 ¥1600E